ALL THESE LUTHERANS

ALL THESE LUTHERANS

Three Paths toward a New Lutheran Church

TODD W. NICHOL

AUGSBURG Publishing House • Minneapolis

ALL THESE LUTHERANS
Three Paths toward a New Lutheran Church

Scripture quotations unless otherwise noted are from the Revised Standard Version of the Bible, copyright 1946, 1952, and 1971 by the Division of Christian Education of the National Council of Churches.

Photos: page 30—Lutheran Theological Seminary at Philadelphia; page 46, A—Lutheran Theological Seminary at Gettysburg, C—Lutheran Theological Seminary at Philadelphia; page 53, A—News Bureau, National Lutheran Council, B, C, D, E—Photographic Collection, LCA Archives; page 70, B—Courtesy of Concordia Historical Institute, St. Louis MO, C—ALC Archives; page 92, A—S. P. Eggan photo, courtesy of George Sverdrup, B—ALC Archives, C—Lutheran Standard; page 102, A, B—Courtesy of Concordia Historical Institute, St. Louis MO; page 110, C—Lutheran Standard.

Library of Congress Cataloging-in-Publication Data

Nichol, Todd W., 1951–
    ALL THESE LUTHERANS.

    Bibliography: p.
    1. Lutheran Church—United States.   2. Christian
union—Lutheran Church.   3. Christian union—United
States.   4. Lutheran Church in America.   5. American
Lutheran Church (1961–   ) 6. Association of
Evangelical Lutheran Churches (U.S.)   7. United States—
Church history.   I. Title.
BX8041.N53   1986   284.1'3   86-3638
ISBN 0-8066-2208-3

Manufactured in the U.S.A.   APH 10-0228

1   2   3   4   5   6   7   8   9   0   1   2   3   4   5   6   7   8   9

To the people
of

Christ English Lutheran Church
Minneapolis, Minnesota
Romans 1:16-17

and

Saint Philip's Lutheran Church
Fridley, Minnesota
1 Peter 2:9-10

CONTENTS

PREFACE

Three Lutheran churches in the United States are talking about forming a new Lutheran church. That makes this a good time to tell family stories. Our stories will help us get acquainted. And they will help us build for the future.

The stories told here are about the long haul toward American Lutheran unity. They tell how Lutherans have planted, divided, and united their churches. They are about large groups and momentous happenings. If lively people and vital events are not mentioned, it is not because they are unimportant. It is to make the plot clear, themes plain, and the stories short.

There are other stories to tell. To meet all the men and women, to sing the hymns, to hear the sermons, to celebrate the Baptisms, to eat and drink at the Lord's Supper, to go to Sunday school, to ride with missionaries, to follow the arguments, to confess the faith—to do all that and so much else with American Lutherans—you need to read a history. We have good ones and they make fascinating reading.

There is a juicy thickness to the American Lutheran past
stored in those fat books.

But this is not a history, and it is not a book for scholars.
This is a collection of stories for church people about how
their churches came to be. The stories are told with the idea
in mind that remembering the past is an important part of
keeping the faith and carrying it into the future.

I am grateful to several friends who helped me with this
little book. It is dedicated with thanks to the congregations
gracious enough to have had me among their pastors.

ALL THESE LUTHERANS
. . . ALL THOSE SYNODS

The humor corner of a Lutheran journal recently ran this anecdote. A couple who were thinking of moving to a new town visited the place and drove by a Lutheran church. When they saw the youth of the congregation having a car wash, one of them shouted out the car window, "What synod are you?" "What's the difference?" the answer shot back. "We all wash cars the same!" It could only happen in America. And only between Lutherans.

It is usually the first question Lutherans ask when they meet each other: "What synod are you?" And their neighbors often ask the same question. If our Methodist or Roman Catholic friends know anything at all about Lutherans it is usually something like this: "There are all these Lutherans with all those synods." If they know anything else about Lutherans it is that, alike as we are, there are differences among us. They may not understand why we differ (sometimes even we forget why), but they know we do.

Some people know that our traditions first came to us from many lands in a multitude of languages. But that is only half the story of our variety. Here in the United States we have spent more than 300 years experimenting with our inheritance, dividing and uniting, while wrestling with the question, What does it mean to be Lutheran in America?

You can't eat fjords

I once asked one of my grandmothers what prompted her to leave home—a village nestled into a lovely cove on a Norwegian fjord—and settle in America. She looked me in the eye and said, "You can't eat fjords."

She spoke for millions. By the time she came to the United States during World War I, it was a tale that had been told over and over again. In hard times, people in Europe would read letters from America where the streets were known to be strewn with gold and pigs were said to somersault into your skillet for sausage. When times got harder yet, when stomachs growled and children cried, they would talk about acquaintances who had already left. They would listen to peddlers of promises and hucksters hawking the hope of a better future. One by one, and family by family they would sit at night, look silently across the room, and then decide to go. Mothers and fathers watched them leave.

"America-fever" is what some Europeans called it. It was a disease of the desperate. It was easy to diagnose and everyone knew its causes. The poor were pushed from their homes for want of food, land, work, and opportunity. Sometimes they left to evade military conscription or for political reasons. Occasionally they left for the chance to think new thoughts. Some left, or were forced to leave, for the sake of religion.

The exodus from Europe began in the 1600s with trickles of people leaving the old countries for the new land. By the

1800s the trickles had turned into rivers. They were still pouring into the United States during the first decades of the 20th century. For 300 years they came, until laws passed in the 1920s restricted immigration to a trickle again.

Push and pull

Europe pushed them out and America pulled them in. There was work to be had. Sometimes it was hard work under brutal conditions for a pittance in pay, but it was work. And there was land. The great spaces of the North American continent made the fenced farms of Europe look tiny. Even the poorest people could dream about owning land in America, and sometimes their dreams came true.

Possibility pulled hard. There was a sense of opportunity in America. The stories about gold and the somersaulting pigs were not true, but the air in America was free. You did not have to be what your mother or your father had been. You could—if you chose, if your luck held, and if you worked hard—be something else. You could think and imagine and dream for yourself in America.

A good fit

There were Lutherans in those rivers of immigrants that poured into the United States. Most of the Lutherans came from northern Europe. That meant they would get along well with the descendants of other Europeans whose fore-bears had arrived earlier. "Yankees," the Lutherans called these people whose ancestors had come from England and Scotland. These were the people who owned the banks, taught in the schools, kept the stores, and held political power. They envisioned the United States as a nation of people like them: white Protestants descended from Anglo-Saxon ancestors. Their notion of America dominated the national imagination for a long time, and for decades most of the people who came after them tried to accommodate themselves to it.

The Lutherans fit the Yankee vision almost perfectly. Almost all of them were white. They were indisputably Protestant. And they were usually political conformists. They generally found it easy to vote with one or another of the large political parties. These Lutherans from northern Europe earned a reputation as steady, industrious people who tried to fit Yankee expectations. Good "Americanizers," they were called. They even had prejudices that fit the prevailing patterns. For example, they were usually violently allergic to certain religions. It did not take long for Scandinavians and Germans to learn to look at Italian Roman Catholics or Polish Jews and mutter about "foreigners." To the Yankees who had gotten there before them, the Lutherans seemed to melt right into the American mix.

By the end of the 19th century, in fact, many Americans thought of the United States as a melting pot. This was illustrated by a little drama played out by students who attended a school for immigrants established by Henry Ford. The first thing immigrant employees who went to work for Ford learned to say in English was, "I am a good American." Later, as students in his compulsory English school, some of them took part in a pantomime with a point. A huge kettle labeled "Melting Pot" stood on the stage. A long column of immigrants in foreign dress and carrying signs identifying their homelands poured into the pot from backstage. At the same time another column poured out, these people dressed like Americans and carrying little American flags.[1] No one could miss the point. For some people, America was a kind of melting pot.

The northern European nationalities seemed to melt easily. As hard as it was for parents who sat listening to their children speak a language they could not understand, and painful as school days were for children who went to public school ashamed of their "foreign" parents, the Germans and Scandinavians did blend in quickly. Before long, little remained to their children and grandchildren but wistful memories of the old countries, special food eaten on holidays, and broken remnants of half-remembered languages used when children were not to hear.

Religion in general

If nationality melted down so easily, what would happen to religion in the melting pot? Would it blend in, too?

The people who wrote the Constitution of the United States had wondered and worried about the same questions. They did not nurse the naive idea that religion and government could be separated. They understood that churches and civil authority would always have business to do with each other. Not far removed from centuries of religious warfare in Europe, they knew the disruptive potential of religion. They wondered how to tame it without killing it.

The framers aimed to do four things about religion when they wrote the Constitution and the Bill of Rights. First, they set out to secure freedom of speech, press, and assembly. Second, they wanted to encourage religious faith because they thought it helped make responsible citizens. (Benjamin Franklin liked this idea so much that he contributed to almost every church that asked him for money!) Third, they insisted that no church be established as a national church. This meant that no church would receive revenues from special taxes, particular privileges not granted to others, or any special recognition or assistance from the federal government. Fourth, they thought that the best way to avoid factional strife among religions was to guarantee free competition among them. They organized religion the way they organized the national economy. It was a daring experiment: a free market in religion.

At first, the churches hardly knew what to make of the experiment. In most of the nations of Europe, a single church had been established. If you didn't belong to the church, you were called a "dissenter" and your church was called a "sect." The idea that a nation could genuinely tolerate more than one church or a variety of faiths had hardly been tried. The American pattern was so innovative that it took the churches a while to invent forms to fit it, but eventually the idea of "denominations" appeared on the scene.

The notion of denominations makes the zesty variety of American religion possible. Any group can lay claim to the truth, work out the shape of a life together, and so make a denomination. No denomination has special privileges. Government and society ask only that all denominations endorse a basic moral consensus. Conflicts—between denominations, within denominations, between denominations and the civil authorities, and between individuals and denominations—are for the courts to arbitrate. Of course, this arrangement has had its problems. Issues like military service, school prayers, and even blood transfusions have brought believers and the body politic into conflict.

But in spite of its occasional problems, denominationalism has gotten into our bones. Most of us have come to think of religion as largely a private matter, but at the same time as a common bond that somehow makes us good citizens. Perhaps only Americans could really appreciate something Dwight Eisenhower once said: "Our government makes no sense unless it is founded in a deeply felt religious faith—and I don't care what it is."[2]

Because of our variety, most of us are profoundly committed to what we call tolerance, although it may be cooperation and agreeableness rather than tolerance that we are really talking about. We have all grown used to the idea that there are many denominations claiming many ways to the truth. This variety has shaped the way we think and the way we experience religion.

Lutheranism in particular

With so many denominations around them, Lutherans have repeatedly had to ask themselves: What does it mean to be Lutheran in America? That has been the big question for Lutherans in the United States. All those synods have been a part of the answer.

In a practical way, denominationalism came easily to those who first brought Lutheranism to our shores. Most of them were used to life in one of the established churches of Europe, but they took to American ways quickly. Their inherited religion placed a high value on obedience to civil authority and social cooperation, and they quickly accepted the American way of doing things. When it came to building churches, they borrowed ideas from their neighbors, adapted ideas from home, and worked out new patterns on their own. With little help from Europe, the Lutheran leaders worked hard to find their own people and gather them into congregations.

Although vast numbers of Lutherans left the fold of their faith when they left Europe, and many joined other groups when they arrived in America, growing Lutheran denominations made their mark early in this country. Lutherans had lots of children and built lots of churches.

With more people arriving from Europe every year and moving to new parts of the country, it was not surprising that Lutheran denominations multiplied. Nationalities and the languages that went with them made differences between Lutherans. Newly arrived Scandinavians wanted to worship with Scandinavians and freshly come Germans with Germans. Passing time also made differences. People who had just arrived often felt more at home with each other than they did with families who had arrived two or three generations earlier. Geography played a part, too. In the days when travel was by foot and horseback and ferry, Ohio seemed as big as a continent. It was natural for Ohio to have its own denomination. Wherever they needed one, Lutherans started what they usually called a *synod*.

There were other reasons for all those synods, deep and divisive reasons. As soon as Lutherans left Europe and their roomy old churches there, they divided over doctrine and piety. They had different notions of what was true and how to express the truth. They had different ideas about experiencing the faith and living the Christian life. What the authority of the state had held together in Europe came apart in America. If you found enough people who agreed with you about doctrine and piety, you could start a synod. If you disagreed with them, you could leave and take as many friends with you as would go and start still another synod. It did not take Lutherans long to discover many answers to the question, What does it mean to be Lutheran in America? Sometimes it seemed as if there were almost as many synods as there were answers to the question.

And now how many?

How many answers? And how many synods? The questions are still open.

For a long time Lutherans in the United States—their numbers reinforced by boatloads of immigrants and biology—planted, multiplied, and divided until there were more synods and churches than almost anyone could keep track of. But about the time of World War I, they discovered that old differences of nationality, chronology, and geography were not so divisive among a people increasingly at home in America. Lutherans began to ask themselves about their differences in doctrine and piety and found that they had enough in common to bring them together in increasingly larger federations and synods. More often than before they called their denominations "churches," a little sign of an important change in thinking.

Several large groups joined hands about the time of World War I, and in the years after World War II steps were taken toward other mergers. By the middle of the 1960s, the great majority of American Lutherans were gathered into three churches: the Lutheran Church in America (LCA), the American Lutheran Church (ALC), and the Lutheran Church–Missouri Synod (LCMS). In the 1970s a group of Missourians left their synod to form the Association of Evangelical Lutheran Churches (AELC).

Three of these churches—the LCA, the ALC, and the AELC—are pondering a merger in the late 1980s. If they have not discovered a common answer to the question, What does it mean to be Lutheran in America? they have recognized enough unity in approaches to the question to talk of building a new church together.

With the momentous question of merger in front of us, it is important for us to share family stories. Our stories will help us get to know each other. They will help us reach toward the future. And they will help us reckon with another and even more important question: What does it mean to be Lutheran in America?

THE LUTHERAN CHURCH IN AMERICA

1962

Prolog

A Danish Christmas

It may have been in Danish that Lutherans first preached and prayed together in North America.

King Kristian IV of Denmark and Norway, like so many other monarchs and adventurers of his time, wanted to discover a northwest passage to the Orient. To find that imaginary keyhole to the East, he sent an expedition to what is now Canada. A Lutheran chaplain sailed with the two Scandinavian ships and conducted services regularly. The sailors suffered terribly during the winter of 1620 in an encampment on Hudson Bay. Their captain penned a poignant description of their Christmas that year: "Holy Christmas Day was celebrated in customary Christian fashion. We had a sermon and Communion; and our offerings to the minister after the sermon were in accord with our means."[1]

They gave the chaplain fur to line his coat against the cold. Warm as his coat may have been, Pastor Rasmus Jensen died sometime later. By Good Friday only five of the crew could sit up for worship. In the end, only the captain and two sailors returned to Scandinavia.

It was a hard beginning.

Dealing with the Dutch

Meanwhile, Dutch sailors and merchants had been exploring the territory of what is now New York since early in the 1600s. They had a permanent settlement there by 1624.

The Dutch authorities intended to permit the public practice of only one faith in their colony: the Reformed Protestantism (a brand of Calvinism) of their homeland. But there were Lutherans in New Netherland from the beginning. Although they were expected to keep their religion to themselves, the Lutherans formed a congregation in the city of New Amsterdam (later called New York) and asked for a pastor. The authorities turned them down, even though Lutherans were permitted to congregate at home in the Netherlands. When a Lutheran pastor finally arrived, he was forbidden to hold services and was eventually deported.

The English take over

In 1664, English warships stood off Manhattan Island and demanded the surrender of the Dutch colony. It fell without firing a shot. Overnight, Dutch New Netherland became English New York.

Under the more tolerant rule of the English, Lutherans fared better than they had under the Dutch. Eventually two Lutheran pastors were sent from the Netherlands to take care of the struggling Lutheran congregations in New York. A momentous event occurred in 1703 when a young German land agent who had come to the colonies, Justus Falckner, was ordained to the public ministry of Word and sacrament. He served seven congregations in New York and New Jersey for 20 years—until he died exhausted. A handful of other pastors labored on.

The Lutherans learned valuable lessons from their experience in New York. They adapted Dutch patterns for organizing their congregations, and under English rule they learned lessons in cooperation that all Christians in America would eventually have to learn. They recognized that the old European ideal of one people, one piece of ground, and one religion was doomed in the new land. Religious variety was the rule from the beginning.

The lessons were important and learned in good time. German Lutherans would soon be arriving by the boatload, but not before some Swedish and Finnish Lutherans had settled in the Delaware Valley. In fact, Justus Falckner had been ordained in a Swedish church by pastors from Sweden.

New Sweden

The little colony along the Delaware was not long in Swedish hands, but while it was, Swedes planted the Lutheran church there. Beginning in 1640, pastors were sent from Sweden to minister to the Scandinavian Lutherans and their descendants. One of the first Swedish pastors was John Campanius, who took care of his own people and befriended the native Americans he met in the Delaware Valley. To spread the gospel among his new friends, he translated Luther's *Small Catechism* for them.

As the children of the early settlers from Sweden and Finland became accustomed to life in the colonies, they grew less and less attached to the church of their forebears. English services were introduced in 1742, and the last pastor sent from Sweden arrived in 1770. Eventually the churches of what had once been New Sweden were absorbed into the Protestant Episcopal Church.

Germans in droves

Meanwhile, Germans were arriving by the thousands. Europeans had warred over German lands for more than a century, and conditions were sometimes awful. In the early 1700s food was scarce, winters were hard, and people were restless. What else to do but leave for America? The Germans had their own versions of familiar stories about the promised land across the ocean. Roasted pigeons were said to fly right into your mouth.

The Germans did not come as colonists; they came as individuals and in privately organized groups. They were arriving in force by 1720. Miserably poor, more than half of those who came sold themselves into a form of term slavery, agreeing to work for a stated number of years in return for passage. Hard as conditions were, the poor Germans continued to come. Attracted to Pennsylvania—by the good advertising of William Penn, a hospitable climate, vaguely familiar geography, and the promise of religious freedom—they settled there and in the other middle and southern colonies.

One moment burns with a special brightness in the story of colonial Lutheranism. In 1731 the Lutherans of the city of Salzburg (in what is now Austria) were expelled by their ruler, a Roman Catholic archbishop, who said he would rather have thorns and thistles in his fields than Protestants in his territory. He gave the Lutherans the choice of recanting and becoming Roman Catholics or of going into exile. Village by village they left. Eventually 30,000 walked north toward the sea. It was an exodus.

They were greeted with joy when they reached Lutheran territory. This is what happened when 500 of the Salzburgers arrived in a Thuringian town:

> As the procession moved into the city, all joined in singing "A Mighty Fortress Is Our God," "I Am a Poor Exile," and other hymns. . . . Townsmen broke ranks to lend a helping hand to the aged by grasping their arms and leading them on their way. Children were taken from the arms of their mothers, were kissed and embraced by the welcoming townsfolk. . . . On the day following, Thursday, religious services were conducted for honored guests and, as was wont, when they departed they were given money and personal apparel.[2]

With help from all over Protestant Europe, many of the Salzburgers eventually settled in Georgia in a place they named Ebenezer.

But most of the Germans were scattered up and down the eastern seaboard—like sheep without shepherds. The Lutherans among them wondered what would become of their church. Their traditions had been formed in Europe. Would they work in America?

An answer to the question calls for a look back at the Reformation and early Lutheranism.

Finishing the Reformation

For the better part of a hundred years after Martin Luther died in 1546, Europe was at war. Lutherans, Roman Catholics, Calvinists, and others fought over religious truth and political power.

Even before Luther died, the Lutherans had been hailed before the emperor to give account of their faith. They made their witness in the *Augsburg Confession,* a brief statement of Evangelical Lutheran belief and practice. Eventually Luther's *Small Catechism* and several other statements of faith were gathered into a collection of confessions, *The Book of Concord*. A later generation of theologians developed an even more elaborate version of Lutheranism in response to controversy in the Lutheran household and attacks from outside. These theologians are sometimes called the "orthodox," because they insisted so strenuously on the teaching of pure doctrine in the church.

Theology was a belligerent business in those days. Lutheran theologians put the Christian message—a lively tale meant for telling and trusting as Luther and his friends had rediscovered—into propositions with sharp points. To help forge their weapons, they borrowed complicated methods and terms from university philosophers. Massively learned and industrious, these theologians earned another name sometimes attached to them: "scholastics." These schoolmasters of the church were doughty defenders of Lutheranism and helped to secure its confession in a dangerous time. Their theology still tells the triumph of God's grace. Christians the world over still read their books and the great Lutheran chorales—"Praise to the Lord" and "Now Thank We All Our God" are two of hundreds—still sing of their faith. There were devout believers and devoted pastors in their number, but in the end their scholasticism was too warlike and too academic to do what theology is supposed to do: help the church tell the gospel.

People and pastors wondered what had happened to the clear sound of the trumpet they had heard at the beginning of the Reformation. They began to think that Lutherans had some unfinished business left to them. They remembered that the early Lutherans had said of their church *ecclesia semper reformanda*—"the church must always be reformed."

It was hard not to be discouraged. The wars were terrible and bloody. Military casualties were in ghastly numbers.

Populations were decimated, farmland was ruined, and economies were destroyed. Morals had suffered, as they always do in wartime. People took refuge in drinking and carousing. Alcohol was consumed in such quantities that cash crops were often taken for making liquor instead of food. If people came to church, they sometimes slept through scholastic sermons they couldn't understand. Often churches stood empty and altars were left bare, their brass melted down for cannon and shot.

Europeans finally made a general peace in 1648. They built the settlement on the principle that whoever controlled the government could choose the religion of a particular territory. Europe settled down to life in the "state" churches we can still recognize in some places today.

This way of life did not satisfy some Lutherans. They were set on waking up the church and renewing the Reformation.

Renewing the Reformation

A pastor named Philip Jacob Spener helped rouse the church. An earnest and devout man who had soaked himself in Luther's theology, he grieved over the church's condition. An invitation to write a new preface to an old book of devotion gave him the opportunity to speak out. His preface was published as a separate volume in 1675 under the title, "Heartfelt Desire for a God-Pleasing Reform of the True Evangelical Church, Together with Several Simple Christian Proposals Looking toward this End."[3] The little book was a sobering look at the state of Lutheranism and a manifesto for reform.

Spener called for renewal of doctrine, worship, and life. He demanded an end to unnecessary theological warfare. He wanted the theologians to climb down from the ramparts and minister to Christ's flock. He asked for clear, simple preaching aimed at the heart. He summoned Christians to repentance, conversion, and moral earnestness. Because it was biblical, his outlook was intensely social and intimately individual.

The message went home. Believers came to repentance and were renewed in their baptismal faith. Congregations awakened. Towns reformed. People gathered in small groups to pray and study and encourage each other in the faith. They stirred one another and those around them to deepen themselves in faith and practice the works of love. A new standard of morality enlivened the church and made itself felt in wider and wider circles.

The Christians caught up in this renewing movement were called Pietists and their cause was called Pietism. It was anything but one more "-ism." Though it grew brittle in time, Pietism in its prime was an affair of the heart. It was faith awake and active in love.

Help from Halle

Fired with enthusiasm for renewal, a friend of Spener's, August Hermann Francke, established a cluster of pietist organizations in the university town of Halle. Francke and his collaborators built, among other things, an orphanage, schools, charitable foundations, and a training center for missionaries. They made Halle a hive of pietist activity and caught the attention of Christians around the world. Even the Puritans of New England, busy on the errand of renewing their own version of the Reformation in America, looked to Halle as an example.

When Lutherans in North America desperately needed pastors, it was natural for them to turn to Halle. And Gotthilf August Francke, who had followed in his father's footsteps as Halle's guiding spirit, knew just the preacher to send: Henry Melchior Muhlenberg.

It was a superb choice. Muhlenberg was immensely gifted, and Halle's Pietism had rehearsed him well for America.

The United Lutheran Church in America

Henry Melchior Muhlenberg

Henry Melchior Muhlenberg arrived in the American colonies in 1742 and plunged into the work of finding Lutherans and helping them organize. Although he was the busy pastor of several congregations, Muhlenberg traveled from the Hudson to the Potomac. He concentrated his work in Pennsylvania, New York, and New Jersey, where he brought together congregation after congregation. Wherever he went, he looked for Lutherans, preached, baptized, confirmed, counseled, comforted, and buried the dead. He was a tireless pastor.

Muhlenberg knew how to make over an old tradition to fit new circumstances. There is a hint of frustration in a remark he once made that in America everything has to be voted on, but he came to terms with the democratic spirit of the colonies.[4] He did not try to use European patterns where he knew they would not do.

Muhlenberg spoke and preached in several languages, and from the first acknowledged the importance of English to the future of American Lutheranism. He gladly cooperated with Lutherans of other nationalities and Christians of other denominations, but did not confuse cooperation with doc-

Henry Melchior Muhlenberg, 1711–1787

trinal compromise. Learned and lively, he combined loyalty to the confessions of the Evangelical Lutheran church with all the vitality of Halle's pietism. A more capable bishop for colonial Lutheranism could hardly be imagined.

The Ministerium of Pennsylvania

Muhlenberg never held the title of bishop, but for a generation he was the acknowledged leader of German-American Lutheranism. He left a rich legacy, not least through his skills as an architect of Lutheran unity. In 1747 he called Lutheran pastors and lay leaders together to organize the church beyond the bounds of its congregations. A meeting was held in August of 1748 in Philadelphia. It could rightly be called the first Lutheran convention in the history of the United States. Six pastors and several lay members of various congregations met to share information about the state of the church, to dedicate a new church building, to approve a liturgy, and to examine and ordain candidates for the ministry. Guests of other confessions were invited to take part in worship.[5]

This first meeting produced an informal organization called "The united preachers of the Evangelical Lutheran congregations of German nationality in these American colonies, especially Pennsylvania." Eventually a constitution was adopted for this body, later familiarly known as the Ministerium of Pennsylvania. The name *ministerium* made sense. In its early years, the efforts of this body were primarily directed at obtaining, educating, and approving candidates for the public ministry of Word and sacrament.

The Ministerium of Pennsylvania was the first Lutheran synod formed in the United States. It set some patterns American Lutherans still follow today.

But the Ministerium was not alone in the field for long. America was too big and Lutherans were too diverse for that. Wherever Lutherans settled, synods were springing up. Like other Americans, Lutherans were soon talking not only of "down" South, but about "out" West and "back" East. By 1820, there were five other synods on the scene: New York, North Carolina, Ohio, Tennessee, and Maryland-Virginia.

Growing pains

Synods were not the only symptom of growing pains. After a pause for the American and French Revolutions, immigrants had begun arriving again. The German Lutherans brought with them new religious ideas from Europe and an attachment to their native tongue. It would be a familiar story for American Lutherans: starting over again with new arrivals.

At the same time, Lutherans who had been in the colonies for a time were asking themselves the question, What does it mean to be Lutheran in America? Christians around them had been swept up into movements—sometimes called rationalism and deism—that preached reliance on human reason as a religion. This led them to regard much of what they found in the Scripture and in the later Christian tradition as disposable historical clutter. Thomas Jefferson, for example, went through his New Testament and clipped out the passages he found offensive to unaided reason.

Some Lutherans sharpened their blades to prune their own tradition. They trimmed liturgies, catechisms, confessions, and constitutions to fit the standards of rationalism. Two events, among many, measured the strength of the rationalist movement among American Lutherans. The Ministerium of Pennsylvania removed mention of the Augsburg Confession and the other confessional documents of the Lutheran tradition from its constitution.[6] And for the children of the church, Frederick Henry Quitman of New York wrote a rationalist catechism far removed from the letter and the spirit of Luther's.[7]

In time, the churches stirred themselves to reckon with rationalism. A surge of religious vitality called the Second Great Awakening brought a return to confidence in revelation—mediated through Scripture—as the source of the Christian gospel. Revivals occurred throughout the churches, and denominations began to cooperate with each other in a variety of efforts ranging from the publishing of Bibles to temperance societies. Energetic efforts were launched in several groups to minimize old confessional differences and unite in mutual efforts.

Lutherans roused themselves, too. They remembered their old reliance on Scripture. Most of them liked the renewed emphasis on the Bible. Some of them sponsored revivals, although opinions were always sharply divided over these "New Measures," as they were called. Many Lutherans participated in the work of interdenominational voluntary organizations and some favored a more vigorous ecumenism. Others were more reserved, but a cooperative spirit prevailed.

General Synod

With cooperation in the wind, leaders of the Ministerium of Pennsylvania thought the time was ripe for Lutherans to reach across synodical lines. They brought forward the idea of a synod of synods.

This General Synod was conceived as an advisory federation, without power to intervene in the internal business of its member synods. No doctrinal platform was proposed for the synod, perhaps to avoid contention at the outset. In 1820, a constitution for the new body was approved.

The General Synod had to struggle to stay alive. From the start, New York had been reserved about participation, and Tennessee had set its face like flint against the new synod. Under the leadership of the formidable Henkel family, the Lutherans of the Tennessee Synod favored the use of the German language and a strong confessional position. The Tennesseans were also suspicious of central authority in the church. But it was the Ministerium of Pennsylvania itself that nearly destroyed the General Synod. Agitation in Pennsylvania for an ecumenical union with churches of the Reformed tradition resulted in Pennsylvania's withdrawal from the General Synod in 1823. With that, the Pennsylvanians abandoned a project they themselves had initiated.

In 1823 only two synods, represented by a handful of delegates, met at the convention of the General Synod. It took some plucky westerners to save it. Led by a young pastor named Samuel Simon Schmucker, a special conference took action that led to the formation of a West Pennsylvania Synod. By adding its weight to the scales, it tipped the balance in favor of the General Synod and saved it from a premature death.

Samuel Simon Schmucker

Schmucker was fired with a passion to find a new way to fit Lutheranism to the American scene. A theologian with a sense for the basics, Schmucker decided that the old Protestant strategy of a return to Scripture alone would help him find a kernel of truth inside traditional husks he could throw out. He borrowed his version of this strategy from neighboring American Protestants, sometimes called "Evangelicals." Hoping that a common front would make ecumenical partnerships possible, he followed the Evangelical lead in laying plans to rebuild American Lutheranism.

Schmucker believed that revising the Lutheran tradition was the best and only way to preserve it in America, and took on himself that task of making the revision he thought necessary.

Meanwhile, Schmucker fought valiantly to give American Lutheranism a stable institutional form. He led the struggle to keep the General Synod alive. To serve the same cause, he was at the forefront of an effort to establish a Lutheran seminary in the United States. The effort succeeded when a seminary was established at Gettysburg, Pennsylvania, in 1826. Schmucker became its first professor.

Civil War

Gettysburg was not a name bathed in blood and hallowed in memory when the new seminary was established there, but even in 1826 rumblings of sectional strife in the United States could be heard.

During the decades before the Civil War, the General Synod grew until it included a majority of American Lutherans in its membership. But it was becoming clear that it would not be an easy task to gather all the Lutherans of the country into one tent. The West was always out there, giving anyone who wanted it elbow room and a place to escape from established institutions. (Schmucker and his friends, remember, had been from *western* Pennsylvania when they invented their new synod.) German-speaking Lutherans were agitating for congregations and synods using their language. More Lutherans were beginning to come from places other than Germany and wanted synods of their own, especially in the upper Midwest. And finally, Lutheranism split down the geographic middle at the time of the Civil War.

In 1862, southern Lutherans departed from the General Synod after a convention passed resolutions condemning the Confederacy. The General Synod also passed resolutions supporting Union sympathizers in the South and implying a harsh judgment of southerners who favored the Confederate cause.[8] The result? Another synod, of course. In 1863 the departing synods formed the General Synod in the Confederate States of America.

The wounds were too deep to heal quickly. Northern and southern Lutherans remained divided after the surrender at Appomattox. After protracted negotiations, several synods reorganized a southern Lutheran federation in 1886: the United Synod of the Evangelical Lutheran Church in the South. The United Synod South existed until 1918 and would play an important part in bringing other Lutheran synods together.

New winds

In the middle decades of the 1800s another change of the religious weather occurred in America. The great revivals had spent themselves, and many Protestants looked for new ways of being religious in America. They rediscovered the importance of their inherited traditions. They learned again about their confessions, the sacraments, and the role of a standing ministry. To put it another way, they rediscovered the richness of their Catholic and Protestant past. The notion of the church as a communion enduring through time and spread out across the world took on new importance as Episcopalians, Presbyterians, Baptists, Methodists, Lutherans, and others recovered a new sense of history and identity.

For Lutherans, this meant an intense engagement with the traditions of the Reformation, the Lutheran confessions, and the theology of the scholastics. The sacraments took on a renewed importance for them as they recovered a sense of the reality of the rebirth given in Baptism and of the vitality of the Lord's real presence in his Supper. They up- held the *Augsburg Confession* and Luther's *Small Catechism* as standards of life and faith for the church. They read again the thick tomes of the Lutheran scholastics. They recovered the riches of Lutheran liturgical traditions. A new sense of identity made them cautious about cooperation with other denominations.

A group of young theologians led the effort to recover the past and put it to work in the present. They translated and wrote tirelessly. Best-known of these young pastors was Charles Porterfield Krauth. He published his masterwork in 1871, an influential book with a revealing title, *The Conservative Reformation and Its Theology.*[9] Even today, worn copies of Krauth's book stand on shelves in Lutheran li- braries and in the study of many a pastor.

Controversy

Krauth had not yet written his great book when contro- versy erupted in the General Synod.

The conservatism of Krauth and his friends was a chal- lenge to the kind of Lutheranism Samuel Simon Schmucker had helped create. By the 1850s, opinion was beginning to lean in the direction of the younger and more conservative leaders. Pennsylvania, so long a bellwether, had moved in a conservative direction and in 1853 had rejoined the Gen- eral Synod along with two other conservative synods. Penn- sylvania did so on the condition that the General Synod require nothing of it that would violate its renewed sense of the old traditions of Evangelical Lutheranism.

The two schools of thought in the General Synod—rep- resented by Krauth and Schmucker—coexisted uneasily un- til 1855. In that year Schmucker published (anonymously, but everyone soon knew he was the author) a booklet titled *Definite Synodical Platform.*[10] The pamphlet was a program outlining a theological foundation for Schmucker's "American Lutheranism." The crucial section of the *Definite Platform* contained a revision of the *Augsburg Confession.* This revision rejected as erroneous five important elements of the *Augsburg Confession:* (1) approval of the ceremonies of the mass or liturgy; (2) private confession and absolution; (3) denial of a divinely instituted obligation to observe the sabbath; (4) rebirth in Baptism; (5) the real presence of Christ's body and blood in the Lord's Supper.

The *Definite Synodical Platform* set the General Synod simmering. The young conservative leaders were adamantly opposed to the kind of Lutheranism advocated in Schmucker's tract. They took to pulpit, print, and convention floors to defend the unaltered *Augsburg Confession* as the standard of Lutheran faith and life.

General Council

As debate between the two schools went on, events provoked a crisis. The young conservatives were dismayed when two new synods—one of which endorsed the *Augsburg Confession* in a qualified way and the other of which had never accepted it at all—were received into the membership of the General Synod. When the latter, new synod was accepted, the delegates from Pennsylvania withdrew from the convention to report to the Ministerium and take counsel.

Things took a new turn in 1864, when Samuel Simon Schmucker retired from his professorship at the Gettysburg Seminary. Charles Porterfield Krauth was the conservative candidate for the post, but another person was elected. The Ministerium of Pennsylvania responded by naming Krauth to the faculty of a new seminary it had just opened in Philadelphia. Pennsylvania then withdrew from membership in the General Synod. It was a classic case of Christian controversy: ideas, people, events, institutions, and causes all in a tangle for the sake of the faith.

After withdrawing, Pennsylvania issued a call to other Lutheran synods, inviting them to join in a union based on adherence to the unaltered *Augsburg Confession*. A meeting of representatives was held in 1866 and approved a statement on faith and church polity drawn up by Krauth.[11] With this statement to guide them, 11 synods in 1867 approved a constitution for a body to be called the General Council of the Evangelical Lutheran Church in North America. In the beginning, the Council was largely made up of eastern Lutherans.

Midwesterners were ambivalent about the General Council. Some midwestern groups had declined the invitation. One withheld action because it wanted to debate four specific points, one joined as a member with voice but not vote, while three joined and then withdrew.

Only one largely midwestern body—the Swedish-American Augustana Synod—took unqualified action to join the Council, but it immediately pressed for discussion and action on controversial issues. Augustana prompted debate that led to the elaboration of the so-called Galesburg Rule.[12] This rule held that Lutheran pulpits and Lutheran altars are to be reserved for Lutheran pastors and Lutheran communicants. Opinion was long divided over how the rule was to be interpreted and enforced.

But with or without collaborators in the Mississippi Valley, the Lutherans of the General Council offered a vigorous answer to the question of Lutheran identity in America. They built a strong and growing church on the foundation of their answer. They stood on an allegiance to the *Augsburg Confession* as the basis of their unity.

Reunion

By 1867, then, the family Henry Melchior Muhlenberg had founded was divided into three branches: the General Synod; the groups on their way to forming the United Synod, South; and the General Council.

But the sense of family never died. In the 1870s, informal meetings between members of the three bodies explored common ground and differences of opinion. The southern Lutherans often seemed to stand in the middle between the two larger groups. The existence of a middle ground was an encouraging sign, and meetings continued in the decades that followed. There were changes over the years in all three bodies, but it was plain that the Lutherans of the General Synod were generally moving toward the confessional position of the General Council.

The three groups also collaborated in developing a liturgy and a hymnal that congregations of all three could use. A liturgy was produced in 1888 and a hymnal in 1917.[13] As the liturgies and hymns of the familiar red and green books—*Service Book and Hymnal* of 1958 and *Lutheran Book of Worship* of 1978—would do for later generations, a common service of worship helped draw Lutherans together across denominational barriers.[14]

In 1917 it was time to celebrate the 400th anniversary of the Lutheran Reformation. A committee had been appointed in 1914 to make arrangements for a joint observance by the General Synod, the United Synod South, and the General Council. Lay members of the committee exceeded their mandate and spurred action when they prepared a resolution calling for organic union of the three bodies. Response from the people of the churches was overwhelming, and plans went forward to unite the three denominations. In 1918, at a great celebration in New York City, the United Lutheran Church in America (ULCA) came into being.

In its constitution, the ULCA extended an invitation to other Lutheran bodies sharing its adherence to the unaltered *Augsburg Confession* to join the new church.[15] From the beginning, the ULCA was a body built in the interest of Lutheran unity. It had also opened its mind to a cautious ecumenism involving Lutherans around the globe and even Christians of other confessions. It brought to the American Lutheran scene a long history of experimenting with the question, What does it mean to be Lutheran in America? It embraced several different answers in its traditions, but stood united on the assertion of the *Augsburg Confession* that "For the true unity of the church it is enough to agree concerning the teaching of the Gospel and the administration of the sacraments."[16]

Partners

Slovaks

Immigrants from Czechoslovakia and Yugoslavia came to the United States in two waves: one during the 30 years or so before World War I and another after the armistice of 1918. The Lutherans among the eastern European immigrants formed a small Slovak Lutheran Synod in 1902. This synod joined the Synodical Conference, a federation of synods of which the Missouri Synod was the largest and most influential member.

The small synod was soon on stormy seas. It found itself entangled in controversies over the practice of communicants registering with their pastors before the Lord's Supper, the proper Christian attitude toward lodges and other fraternal societies, whether to use an older or a newer hymnal, and altar fellowship. These debates splintered the synod and some congregations. Only about half of the congregations of the synod remained in its fellowship when the storms subsided.

Another synod was almost inevitable, and the Slovaks were true to American Lutheran form. Many of the congregations that broke with the synod (along with others that had never joined it) formed the Slovak Zion Lutheran Synod in 1918. Its congregations stretched along the industrial belt reaching from New England to Wisconsin.

In 1920 the Slovak Zion Synod entered the United Lutheran Church in America.

Icelanders

Estimates vary, but some say that as many as 20,000 people emigrated from Iceland—a vast number from a country whose population was 70,000 when the emigration began.

The Icelanders settled mainly in Canada and the northwestern part of the United States. Lutherans in their number organized the Icelandic Evangelical Lutheran Synod in America in 1885. The synod was small and struggled for life, but like its larger counterparts it was invigorated by lively personalities and theological controversy.

Although it shared a common bond with Scandinavian groups in the Midwest, it had early ties with the General Council. The Icelandic Synod joined the ULCA in 1940.

Finns

When Finnish Lutherans first came to the upper midwest they cooperated with other Scandinavians in gathering congregations and forming synods. The Finns settled in the northern states, with a large group making a home for itself in the mining country of northern Michigan.

Congregations were first gathered together after the American Civil War, but it was not until 1890 that the

Finnish Evangelical Lutheran Church of America was organized. It was led by a quartet of gifted and energetic pastors.

Governed by a consistory of pastors and divided by clashing convictions, the Suomi Synod, as it was familiarly called, had a turbulent youth. Strong personalities, hard times, and controversies with communist organizers all agitated the little synod. During early decades of growth it managed to establish a college and seminary before experiencing difficult years of declining membership in the 1920s and 1930s. In later years membership again grew. The Suomi Synod was always strongly marked by its Finnish origin. Not until 1958 did subscriptions to the English church paper of the synod exceed those of its Finnish counterpart.

Like the Icelanders, the Finnish Lutherans were kin to the other Scandinavian-American Lutherans they met in the upper Midwest. Nevertheless, events drew the Lutherans of the Suomi Synod close to the Lutherans of the ULCA after World War I.

Danes

If you spend much time among the neighbors of Danish American Lutherans for long, you will usually hear somebody say something about "Happy" Danes and "Sad" Danes or "Holy" Danes.

The "Happy" Danes inherited their traditions from a movement begun in the Church of Denmark by Nikolai Frederik Severin Grundtvig. As a young man, Grundtvig had awakened to faith and denounced the Danish church for sleepiness and doctrinal laxity. A keen sense of the vitality of the gospel led him to the belief that the Apostles' Creed was a living word from the mouth of Christ that preceded the preaching of Scripture both in time and importance. A passionate patriot, Grundtvig blended Danish culture and Christianity into an integrated and positive view of life. He is especially remembered for his beautiful hymns and for establishing folk schools for the young people of Denmark.

Grundtvig's spiritual descendants in the United States continued the tradition of celebrating God's living Word spoken in the Creed and "contained," as they liked to say, in the Bible. They worked to preserve a sense of Danish culture in America and sponsored Danish folk schools for their children. Under their starched ruffs and black frocks, the Grundtvigian pastors were a lively crew of clerics. Anticipating many themes prominent in 20th-century Christianity, they were vigorous advocates of what today would be called "wholeness." They argued that you could not understand Christianity if you did not first grasp what it is to be a human being in a culture that has a history.

In 1872, Grundtvigian pastors from Denmark started a Church Mission Society that in 1874 became the Danish Evangelical Lutheran Church. In 1887 the people of the Danish Evangelical Lutheran Church established a seminary and, like other Lutherans before them, soon learned that theological schools were hothouses for controversy. The seminary divided over Grundtvigianism. The outcome was predictable: yet another synod. The anti-Grundtvigian group departed to join others in forming a new coalition that would eventually become the United Danish Evangelical Lutheran Church.

The Danish Evangelical Lutheran Church continued on. In time, the church added "of America" to its name, but for decades it sustained and developed an American version of the traditions of N. F. S. Grundtvig and the Church of Denmark. Even when it changed its name again and became the American Evangelical Lutheran Church (AELC), this denomination had a strong Danish stamp to it. As time went on, the theological outlook of the Danish AELC and lingering antagonisms between it and the group that had earlier separated from it, made it a natural—and happy—partner of the ULCA.

Swedes

In the 100 years between 1820 and 1920, Sweden sent more than a million of its daughters and sons to the United States. Almost all of them were Lutherans.

They came from an ancient church that had often been challenged by renewing movements. A vibrant pietism stirred Swedish Lutheranism in the 19th century, and revivals swept the countryside, especially in the province of Småland, from which many of the immigrants to America came. When Swedish Lutherans who had experienced revivals at home came to America, they were no strangers to the kind of religion they met there. It was easy for them to become Methodists and Baptists and Episcopalians.

Sometimes it seemed as if no one at home cared, especially when the bishops did not stir themselves to send pastors. Their delay was costly. The upper Midwest was already home to many Swedes when a pastor finally arrived. He was Lars Paul Esbjörn, remembered by Swedish-Americans as the "Prairie Shepherd." With little help coming from Sweden, Esbjörn turned to the Congregational American Home Missionary Society for assistance. Lutherans from the East helped, too.

Esbjörn traveled the country to find Swedish Lutherans and raise money. He battled proselytizing preachers of other denominations and helped the Swedish Lutherans organize congregations. Esbjörn was heartened a few years later when three other pastors joined him: Tuve Nilsson Hasselquist, Erland Carlsson, and Eric Norelius. Along with the men

Samuel Simon Schmucker
1799–1873

Lars Paul Esbjörn
1808–1870

Charles Porterfield Krauth
1823–1883

and women who gathered themselves into the first congregations, these heroic pastors are remembered as the founders of the Augustana Synod.

In 1851, Swedes and Norwegians joined English-speaking Lutheran congregations and pastors in founding the Synod of Northern Illinois as a district of the General Synod. Several years later, Esbjörn became Scandinavian professor at the Lutheran college and seminary ambitiously named "Illinois State University" and sponsored by two Illinois synods. The arrangement never worked well. Esbjörn felt put upon by having to teach subjects other than theology, and soon accused his colleagues of being unorthodox.

In 1860, Esbjörn led the Scandinavian students out of the Illinois school, and the Scandinavians withdrew from the Synod of Northern Illinois. The same year Swedish Lutherans collaborated with Norwegians in forming the Scandinavian Evangelical Lutheran Augustana Synod of North America. The name "Augustana" in the title was important. *Confessio Augustana* is the Latin name for the *Augsburg Confession*. The use of the name "Augustana" indicated the intention of the Scandinavians to take the *Augsburg Confession* as the doctrinal standard of their church. In this they were in agreement with their Norwegian friends. Although the connection between the Swedes and the Norwegians was a happy one, the two groups went their own ways in 1870.

The Augustana Synod became a unique ingredient in the American Lutheran mix. It combined a careful confessionalism with a deep piety and a rigorous moral code. Because it had strong congregations in both regions, Augustana knew the experience of life in both the East and the Midwest. Early experiments in ecumenical cooperation encouraged it in cautious cooperation with other Lutherans and Christians of different denominations. It suited Augustana's history well when it became a member of the General Council in

FORMING THE LCA, 1960–1962

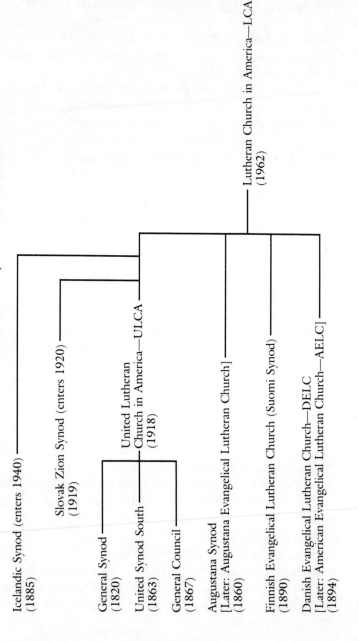

Icelandic Synod (enters 1940) (1885)

Slovak Zion Synod (enters 1920) (1919)

United Lutheran Church in America—ULCA (1918)

Lutheran Church in America—LCA (1962)

General Synod (1820)

United Synod South (1863)

General Council (1867)

Augustana Synod [Later: Augustana Evangelical Lutheran Church] (1860)

Finnish Evangelical Lutheran Church (Suomi Synod) (1890)

Danish Evangelical Lutheran Church—DELC

American Evangelical Lutheran Church—AELC] (1894)

1867, even if the relationship was not without its bumpy moments. It knew the traditions of the ULCA intimately from a long experience of cooperation, and—when theological developments went apace and in the same directions in the two bodies—it was not surprising that Augustana and the ULCA thought alike about Lutheran unity in the 20th century.

Unity

World War I

World War I was a challenge to Lutherans in the United States. When a hysterical patriotism turned against everything German, sauerkraut was renamed "liberty cabbage" and Lutherans were suddenly suspect. Silly stories were circulated about Lutheran loyalty pledges to the German Kaiser, and the barns of farmers with German names were streaked with yellow paint. Even Scandinavians were harassed. The slogan of the day was "100% Americanism," and people were not always careful about sorting out "foreigners." The trauma was momentary, but not easy. World War I hurried Lutherans out of European ways and helped to bring them together.

The prospect of gold and silver stars on service flags prompted Lutheran leaders to organize a National Lutheran Commission for Soldiers' and Sailors' Welfare to see to the spiritual needs of Lutherans in the military. Thirteen Lutheran bodies were represented.

The experience of cooperation in an emergency and the urgent needs of Lutherans in war-torn Europe spurred American Lutheran leaders to consider a permanent organization, and late in 1918 the National Lutheran Council

(NLC) was formed. Included in the organization were the three bodies on their way to becoming the United Lutheran Church in America and several largely midwestern bodies: the Augustana Synod; the two Danish churches; the Icelandic Synod; the Lutheran Free Church; the Norwegian Lutheran Church; and the Buffalo, Iowa, and Ohio Synods.

Although there were problems, the Lutherans of the Council discovered they could work together in an emergency. When the war was over, they wondered if they could do other things together, too. In 1919 and 1920, therefore, representatives of the member churches held meetings in Chicago to discuss theology and lay a foundation for future cooperative efforts. Discussions revealed two approaches in the Council to the question of Lutheran cooperation.

On the one hand, President H. G. Stub of the Norwegian Lutheran Church presented a set of propositions soon named the Chicago Theses.[17] Stub's theses represented a conservative, midwestern Lutheran theology. Especially important were his use of the term *inerrant* to describe the text of the Bible and his insistence on including detailed statements on questions disputed by the midwestern churches. Underlying Stub's presentation was the idea that cooperation demands adherence to the Lutheran confessions *and* agreement on disputed questions of theology.

On the other hand, President Frederick H. Knubel and Professor Charles M. Jacobs of the United Lutheran Church had prepared a statement titled, "The Essentials of the Catholic Spirit in the Church," arguing for a more flexible approach to cooperation.[18] Knubel and Jacobs differed with Stub. They worked from the idea that adherence to the Lutheran confessions was a sufficient basis for cooperation. They did not think, for example, that disagreement over

questions about the inspiration of Scripture or its inerrancy—though important—ought to separate Lutherans or ob-
struct cooperation between them.

Opinion remained divided after the meetings in Chicago,
but the National Lutheran Council continued to serve as a
cooperative agency for American Lutherans.

Division and steps toward unity

In the 1930s a group of midwestern Lutheran churches—
each of which already belonged to the National Lutheran
Council—created another federation, the American Lutheran Conference. The ULCA was not consulted about the
formation of this body and was not invited to join. When
the Chicago Theses presented by Stub in 1919 were incor-
porated into a theological rationale for the formation of the
Conference (a new set of statements usually called the Minneapolis Theses) it was plain that opinions about cooperation and the way toward American Lutheran unity were
still divided.[19]

There were hurt feelings over the formation of the American Lutheran Conference. This was made clear by Frederick
Knubel in a speech to a Conference convention.[20] The ir-
ritation caused by this midwestern activity did not, however,
prevent the ULCA from exploring possibilities of unity with
the Augustana Synod and with the American Lutheran
Church, a church formed by three German-American bodies
in 1930. Augustana felt that the time was not ripe for action,
but remained interested in conversation with the ULCA.
Discussion with the American Lutheran Church faltered
over questions about Scripture. Agreements were reached,
but different approaches to inspiration and inerrancy created
tensions in both churches. Discussions between the ULCA
and the Missouri Synod were difficult, producing more fric-
tion and frustration than cooperation.

World War II

"It takes a war to bring the Lutherans together," some said. World War II at least scrambled them up, even if it did not exactly bring American Lutherans together. They cooperated abroad and at home. Chaplains did not ask about synods on the battlefields and neither did lonely soldiers who visited canteens looking for hot coffee and news from home. Back in the United States, Americans began moving around the country as never before, and often simply joined the nearest Lutheran congregation or joined any Lutherans they met in creating one.

Like the war that preceded it, World War II demanded special cooperation from Lutherans. And when peace returned, relief work in Europe called forth massive collaborative efforts. At the same time, the rebuilding of global Lutheran ties in the new Lutheran World Federation helped American Lutherans get to know one another as well as European Lutherans.

American Lutheran unity was in the air after World War II. What form would it take? Federation of the bodies cooperating in the NLC? Merger? Or mergers?

Mergers

In January of 1949, representatives of churches belonging to the National Lutheran Council met to discuss Lutheran unity. After considering the alternatives, these representatives asked their churches to answer two questions. First, were they ready to approve the idea of organic unity? Second, were they prepared to transform the NLC into a federation as a step on the way to unity? Four churches in effect said no to both questions and went on to form the American Lutheran Church in 1960–1963.

Frederick Herman Knubel
1870–1945
First president ULCA

Franklin Clark Fry
1900–1968
President ULCA,
First president LCA

Malvin H. Lundeen
b. 1901
President Augustana

Raymond W. Wargelin
b. 1911
President FELC

Anders Ejnar Farstrup
1909–1984
President AELC

The four church body presidents at the time of the merger that formed
the LCA were Franklin Clark Fry (ULCA), Malvin H. Lundeen (Augustana), Raymond W. Wargelin (FELC), and Anders Ejnar Farstrup
(AELC).

Two churches said yes to the questions before the National Lutheran Council. As the 1950s opened, steady agitation for merger came from the ranks of Augustana and the ULCA. In 1954 the two churches issued an invitation to 14 bodies to join talks considering unity. The American Evangelical Lutheran Church and the Suomi Synod accepted the invitation. The four churches moved to unite and in 1962 created the Lutheran Church in America (LCA).

What does it mean to be Lutheran in America?

What kind of answer did the new Lutheran Church in America give to the old question of Lutheran identity?

The LCA brought together traditions originating with immigrant Danes, Finns, Germans, Icelanders, Slovaks, and Swedes. The Lutherans who bore these traditions with them had come to the United States over three centuries. They began arriving during the earliest moments of the colonial experience and kept coming until the gates were all but closed in the 1920s. By 1962 even the traditions that had come latest were profoundly altered by the experience of life in the United States. English was the first language of almost all of these Lutherans and the only language of most of them. The families of almost all the people who belonged to the ULCA had long been in the United States, and even in the other churches—closer to their ethnic roots—the collective memory of the European past had begun to turn to nostalgia. The name of the new church was apt in more ways than one. These Lutherans were at home "in America."

The Lutherans of the new LCA also have a long history of reckoning with doctrine. Henry Melchior Muhlenberg brought Halle's Pietism, Samuel Simon Schmucker had revised the Lutheran tradition for America, revivalists and conservative theologians took a hand in shaping it, and in the 20th century new approaches appeared. Particularly important were historical criticism of the Bible and new trends in ecumenism. About mid-century, theologians of the churches preparing to become the LCA jumped feet first into the diversity of contemporary theology.

In public piety, in their faithfulness and practice at public worship, the Lutherans of the LCA are much like other Lutherans. A strong liturgical movement has made itself felt in some circles. Revivals are little heard of anymore, but new patterns of renewal have taken their place in the 20th century. Traditions of the Scandinavian and Slovak synods still prevail in some places. Inherited moral codes—prohibiting dancing, smoking, card-playing, and the use of alcohol—are observed by some families, especially those standing in the traditions of Augustana, but their numbers are smaller than in earlier generations. Today the once touchy question of lodge membership for Lutherans is not often debated.

How does it make a church?

In its constitution the LCA builds on old traditions. The Bible, the ancient creeds of the church, and the Lutheran confessions are its platform. The Scriptures are acknowledged as "the norm for the faith and life of the church" and described as ". . . the divinely inspired record of God's redemptive act in Christ, for which the Old Testament prepared the way and which the New Testament proclaims." The constitution says of the *Small Catechism* and the *Augsburg Confession* that they are "true witnesses to the Gospel." The other confessions are "further and valid interpretations" of these two primary confessions. A commitment to a cautious but aggressive ecumenism is at work in an important statement about unity and fellowship. The LCA "acknowledges as one with it in faith and doctrine all churches that likewise accept the teachings of these symbols."[21] In this statement, LCA makes plain that it has an ecumenical vision of Christian unity. This spacious vision is a crucial part of its answer to the question, What does it mean to be Lutheran in America?

The church that stands on this platform defines itself as a body of congregations and a ministerium. In this definition it reaches back to traditions first developed by Muhlenberg and his colleagues, who organized a "ministerium" that eventually became a "synod." An emphasis on the ministry as integral to the definition of the church is characteristic of the LCA in a way not familiar to other American Lutherans.

The synods of the LCA are not synods in the classical sense of the term, but they are important regional expressions of its life. In and through their synods the people of the LCA do the business of the whole church. They make their meetings festive occasions. It is an especially important moment in the synod's meeting when candidates, who have been approved and prepared under the supervision of the synod, are ordained to the public ministry of Word and sacrament. Because the clergy are intrinsic to the definition of the church in the LCA, not only representatives of the congregations, but all clergy (whether or not they serve congregations) attend meetings of the synod.

Like most other Protestant churches of the United States, the LCA is structured like a large corporation, with boards, executives, and staffs accountable to the constituency through periodic national meetings. As one of its members has said in a book about the formation of the LCA, there is a formidable bureaucracy in his church, and the old feeling of family is harder to find than it was in the smaller churches of an earlier era.[22] Because of the structure and size of their church, national and synodical leaders of the LCA have often been excellent managers and administrators as well as pastors and theologians. Franklin Clark Fry—sometimes called "Mr. Protestant," and the LCA's first president—was an extraordinary example of this combination.

If the intimacy of a small family is missing, the vigor of a big one is not. The LCA is a denomination of a little under three million members in more than 6000 congregations.[23] It has congregations across the country, but most of its people live east of the Mississippi River. The old bastion of Pennsylvania is still thick with the Lutherans of this church, and there are large contingents in Minnesota and Illinois as well.

How has the LCA answered the question, What does it mean to be Lutheran in America? It has not given a single answer. The traditions behind this church permit experimentation with a variety of responses. Its answers to the question grow out of a long experience of American life. They come from ethnic variety, practice at partnerships, commitment to the Lutheran confessions and ecumenical cooperation, engagement with the changing course of Christian thought, a variety of pieties, and a spacious ecumenical vision.

THE AMERICAN LUTHERAN CHURCH
1960–1963

Awakening and Confession

Rational religion

When Martin Luther stood before the Emperor Charles
V at the Diet of Worms, he said:

> Unless I am convinced by the testimony of the Scriptures or
> by clear reason . . . I am bound by the Scriptures I have
> quoted and my conscience is captive to the Word of God. I
> cannot and I will not retract anything, since it is neither safe
> nor right to go against conscience.[1]

It was an appeal to the authority of Scripture and to the
integrity of reason and conscience.

When philosophers and scientists probed new frontiers
in the years after the Reformation, they often cited Luther's
appeal to reason and conscience but pushed aside what he
had said about the Scriptures. At first they worked from the
idea that reason and the Christian religion offered comple-

mentary approaches to the truth. But after a time they began to argue that reason alone was sufficient for an enlightened and moral life. The extreme among them discarded religion for reason.

Most ordinary people kept the faith they had learned from their mothers and fathers, but the Lutheran pastors of Germany and Scandinavia had absorbed the new ideas about reason and religion from their teachers in the universities. The pastors continued to ply their traditional trade, but used the practice of religion to indoctrinate their flocks in the new creed of rationalism. This was puzzling to the people of the church. They scratched their heads over what they were hearing from their preachers.

The Lutheran confessions were regarded as antique commentaries on squabbles best forgotten. The sacraments were pushed to the edges of church life. Confession and absolution were set aside. Sermons degenerated into discourses on good behavior or practical advice on a multitude of topics. After a while the church nodded off to sleep under preaching like this.

Royalty and revolutions

Royalty and revolutions were as troubling as rationalism.

In the large German kingdom of Prussia, the Calvinist King Frederick William III used the 300th anniversary of the Reformation in 1817 to declare that henceforth the Lutheran and Calvinist churches in his domain were to be united in one church, to be called the "Prussian Church of the Evangelical Union." With a stroke of the royal pen, a Calvinist monarch sentenced the Lutheran churches to death in their German homelands. At first the union was intended to be a voluntary arrangement, but in succeeding years oppressive measures were taken to enforce the king's wishes and unite the churches.

Even more demanding challenges emerged. The modern city and the industrial revolution were new facts of life that put huge questions to the churches. The churches were slow to come to terms with the changing situation. But while churches tried to ignore the reality of metropolis and machine, Karl Marx did not. The communist movement appeared on the scene as one answer to the demands of the new order and as an effective competitor to Christianity. Other socialist alternatives appeared as well. When Germany was shaken by revolution in 1848, the churches trembled and fumbled an opportunity, despite the best efforts of a few visionary leaders. New circumstances and old memories of the excesses of the French Revolution prompted some politicians and Lutheran leaders to take a reactionary posture.

As if social and political revolutions were not enough for the churches to worry about, a scientific revolution challenged old assumptions about the earth and its creatures. Experiment and theory opened vast new worlds in a few short years. Most challenging of all, Darwinism raised the question of the human animal's origin and destiny.

All this turmoil meant that people would have new questions to ask about the Bible. In search of answers, Christian scholars began to uncover evidence—taken from the pages of Scripture itself—that the Bible had been written over a long period of time, that it contained many kinds and layers of literature from a variety of sources, and that it had been put together by editors in a multitude of times and places. The theologians seemed to be in revolt against long established certainties. By the end of the 1800s, historical criticism had shaken the faith of many believers.

Awakening

Just when rationalism seemed to have overcome the churches in the beginning of the 1800s, strong voices called the church to rouse itself to faith. These preachers thought the people of the church were dead in their sins and called its pastors to task for forgetting the gospel. It was high time, they said, for the church to wake up. People listened to them, repented, and believed.

The story of one of these awakeners can stand for them all. Hans Nielsen Hauge was a farmer's son who became an apostle to Norway. As a young man, he experienced a spiritual breakthough to a deep faith. Convinced that he had news to share, he walked the length and breadth of Norway to preach the gospel. He was persecuted by the authorities, but they could not silence his message. He was jailed 10 times and his health was broken, but a movement of friends sustained the awakening in Norway. They honeycombed the country with prayer and preaching. In the Church of Norway you can still hear the echo of Hauge's voice.

Throughout the 19th century, awakenings like the one Hauge started in Norway swept across Germany and Scandinavia. The works of the awakeners still follow after them in the churches of those lands. The awakenings lent Lutheranism new life wherever they touched it.

Confession

Once awakened, Lutherans rediscovered the riches bequeathed to them in their tradition. They began to read Luther, the Lutheran confessions, and the Lutheran scholastics with new interest. Rummaging in the family attic, they found their experience of faith confirmed and corroborated by the traditions of early Lutheranism.

A new sense of identity and integrity took root among Lutherans. In Prussia the Lutheran pastor Klaus Harms republished Luther's 95 Theses and added 95 more of his own for good measure. Harms's theses speak the mind of a revitalized Lutheranism. Of rationalism, one says, "When reason touches religion it casts away the pearls and plays with the empty shells."[2] Another thesis was directed against the Prussian Union. It is a scornful lampoon of the king's plans and a warning of things to come.

> The Lutheran Church is to be treated like a poor maiden who is to be made rich through marriage. Be sure that you do not perform the ceremony over Luther's bones. This will restore them to life, and then woe to you![3]

Harms and others were steadfast in their opposition to the Prussian Union. When the government required the use of a prescribed liturgy and infringed on consciences with other stipulations, the Lutheran opposition stiffened its resistance. Congregations were fined and pastors were jailed. Some Lutherans chose exile rather than conformity. Many of them came to the United States.

Buffeted by rationalism, royalty, and revolutions, the awakeners and confessors of the Lutheran church looked to their theologians for help in proclaiming the gospel. Like people who braid rugs, the theologians worked out new patterns with old materials. They built a theology and a way of life for the church that united the vitality of the awakenings with the stablity of confessional Lutheranism. A few of them were guardedly open to the new historical approach to the Bible. Most of them assumed the inspiration and infallibility of Scripture, and they relied on its authority to undergird both experience and confession. With the Bible underneath them, old theological traditions behind them, and renewing experience to enliven them, these thinkers—sometimes called "restoration" or "repristination" theologians—were able exponents of Lutheranism in turbulent times.

A Lutheran Zion

When Lutherans began settling in the American Midwest during the middle of the 1800s, they brought with them a potent mix of awakening and confession. Arriving in the United States, they reveled in their freedom to build a Lutheranism to their liking. Like Puritans and Pietists before them, they discovered that America was a good place to finish a Reformation they thought had been repeatedly thwarted in Europe. An ocean away from all they feared in Europe, they turned to their traditions to refresh their imaginations and drew deeply from the pictures and promises of the Scriptures. They often spoke of building a Lutheran Zion in America.

The pioneers who built the congregations and synods of midwestern Lutheranism took to denominationalism as if they had been born to it. They shook off the traditional connection to the state like so much dust from their shoes. When it came to building churches, some leaned more heavily on the experience of awakening than on the stability of confession. Others rested more easily on the foundation of confession than in the experience of renewing faith. But all of them knew the reality of both awakening and confession. Out of the stuff of both they built into reality their vision of a Lutheran Zion in America. And in the experience of awakening and the stability of confession they hoped to find the definition of their unity.

Building Zion

Moving west

Even before the American Revolution, white explorers and settlers were moving west. In time, paths were marked, roads were cut, rivers were charted, farms were cleared, and settlements grew up. President Thomas Jefferson sent explorers to the edge of the great, shaggy continent, and soon restless Americans were moving all over it. Lines were drawn, townships were established, and year after year territories declared themselves ready to join the Union as states.

There were Lutherans among those who walked and rode west. They took the church with them because they were the church.

Joint Synod of Ohio

When Ohio joined the Union in 1803 as its 17th state, Lutheran congregations had already established themselves there. The congregations had gathered on their own. They met for worship with reading, prayer, and singing. Yet they missed the ministry of pastors properly prepared to preach and administer the sacraments. Stretched to its limits, the Ministerium of Pennsylvania sent licensed preachers and pastors when it could, but their numbers were few and the field was immense.

Still, the congregations gathered and the itinerant preachers rode out to find them. One of them was John Stauch who was licensed by the Ministerium to preach in 1794 and ordained 10 years later. Stauch's career took him across the Alleghenies and deep into Ohio. It was a rigorous life on the circuit of his preaching places. Here are some entries from his diary of 1806 and 1807:

December 6. Found three German families that know of Jesus. Rode eight miles. 80 cents.

January 4. Preached on John 3:16. Baptized 6 children. There are people here who wish to go to heaven, but few who wish to become pious. Rode six miles.

At the end of his journey, he looked back:

If I have in my haste counted aright, I travelled in all 122 days, preached 67 times, baptized 212 children, covered 1301 miles, and received $28.27.[4]

In a sly moment Stauch once said that he thought it was worth the days in the saddle and the nights out in the open with his head on a stone, because ". . . any of us would be willing to take up with Jacob's pillow if we might but have Jacob's dreams."[5] He may never have seen the angels, but he and a host of other circuit riders did see a church grow up around them.

By 1812, the Ohio congregations were able to organize a special conference of the Ministerium of Pennsylvania. They elected Stauch as their president. In 1818 further steps were taken toward independence when pastors and lay delegates organized the General Conference of the Evangelical Lutheran Preachers of the State of Ohio. Stauch was again elected president. This conference changed its name in 1825 to become the Evangelical Lutheran Synod of Ohio and Adjacent States. Some years later, when the synod divided into eastern and western regions, it added the adjective "Joint" before the term "Synod." Ever afterward its people called it the "Joint Synod."

The early Ohioans—Stauch among them—brought to the frontier the mild pietism of Muhlenberg and the Ministerium of Pennsylvania. In time, however, German immigrants to the Ohio country insisted on the more conservative Lutheranism of the 19th century. They worked changes in the Joint Synod, making it more conservative and self-consciously Lutheran. The German immigrants also brought their native language to Ohio and so made that synod bilingual for many years. Ohio's mind was made up and its temper set by the 1840s. Its congregations would embody a German-American version of the conservative Lutheranism of awakening and confession.

Buffalo Synod

Johannes Andreas August Grabau was one of the Lutheran pastors who defied the king of Prussia and opposed the Union of Lutheran and Calvinist churches. Pastor of the Saint Andreas congregation in the city of Erfurt, Grabau was a thorn in the side of the government and the ecclesiastical authorities. He was suspended from his pastorate and, during a long struggle with officialdom, was jailed, escaped, and jailed again. Finally he was permitted to emigrate and take dissident Lutherans with him.

The congregation in Erfurt and another group of Lutherans in Magdeburg left for the United States in midsummer 1839. When they arrived, a small group stayed in New York City and Albany, a larger group went on to Buffalo, and a sizable contingent, under the leadership of Heinrich von Rohr from Magdeburg, pressed on to settle in Wisconsin. The original colonists were later joined by other German immigrants.

Under Grabau's leadership, the Prussian colony was strictly confessional in doctrine and authoritarian in church government. At Grabau's insistence, considerable power was vested in the clergy and in Grabau himself as *Senior* of the ministerium. Under the rigorous regime of the pastors, a stern church discipline sometimes included the practice of excommunication.

Controversy erupted in the little group of Prussians when those who had gone on to Wisconsin without a pastor asked a lay member of the colony to preach and administer the sacraments until a regular pastor could come to them. Alarmed by this, Grabau dispatched a pastoral letter to the group reprimanding it for this action and explaining his high notion of the ministerial office. When this letter came to the attention of the group of Saxon Lutherans who had settled in the Mississippi Valley and were on their way to becoming the Missouri Synod, a sharp clash occurred between Grabau and the Missourians. The Saxons from Missouri objected to the hierarchical practices of the Prussians. The Missourians preferred a more congregational form of church government and held that the authority of ministers was transferred to them by the congregations they served. The controversy simmered for years.

In 1845 Grabau called together 18 lay members of the congregations and three other pastors to join him in founding a synod for the Prussian dissidents in America. Some of the pathos of their story is packed into the name they chose for the new body: Synod of the Evangelical Lutheran Church Emigrated from Prussia. It was familiarly known as the "Buffalo Synod."

Conflict was inevitable in a synod so tightly ruled. Disputes between Grabau and other pastors as well as dissatisfaction with the rigorous church discipline practiced in the synod shattered the unity of the small body. At one point, Grabau was deposed from his office as *Senior* and tried by an ecclesiastical court. The wrangling Lutherans of Buffalo soon went separate ways: some to Missouri, others to another midwestern body, and some stayed with Grabau. The pastor from Prussia kept the little Buffalo Synod alive in the moment of crisis and it survived, although it never grew large.

Iowa Synod

Wilhelm Loehe was another German pastor in trouble with the authorities. A promising young man and a powerful preacher, his sermons drew crowds until his superiors required him to step down from the prestigious pulpits he had occupied. His preaching, the authorities said, was too vehemently Lutheran. He was exiled to the sleepy Bavarian village of Neuendettelsau.

The world came to him at Neuendettelsau. And from there he sent preachers around the globe. In between his duties as a parish pastor and the pursuit of his avocation as a liturgical scholar, he found time to make the little village a flourishing center for missionary activities. When Loehe saw an appeal for help written by a traveling missionary for the Ministerium of Pennsylvania, F. C. D. Wyneken, his attention was riveted on America. He decided to send missionaries to take care of the Lutherans and to evangelize Native Americans.

Little came of the work with Native Americans, but among the Germans Loehe's emissaries were more successful. Connections were made with the Ohio Synod, and by 1846 the missionary Wilhelm Sihler had established a practical seminary at Fort Wayne, Indiana. In 1852 another school, this one for teachers, was opened in Michigan. But trouble loomed.

Loehe wondered whether the confessional moorings of the Ohio Synod were secure enough and criticized the Ohioans for allowing the use of English. Loehe—who never

John Stauch
1762–1845

J. A. A. Grabau
1804–1879

Wilhelm Loehe
1808–1872

came to America himself—did not believe that German Lutherans could speak their faith in any tongue but their native
German. If these things were not troublesome enough, the
missionaries from Neuendettelsau found themselves caught
between Buffalo and Missouri in their controversy over the
ministry. On the one hand, the congregational polity of
Missouri looked to Loehe like American mob rule and, on
the other hand, the rule of the ministerium in Buffalo
seemed unnecessarily authoritarian.

Eventually a small group of Loehe's people moved to
Iowa in 1853 to make a fresh start. In Dubuque they built
a teacher's seminary that they soon transformed into a seminary for pastors. They endured terrible poverty in the early
years, but they survived. The missionaries were heartened
when reinforcements arrived from Neuendettelsau in 1854.
In the same year they organized the Iowa Synod, and, in
following years—steadily reinforced by arrivals from
Loehe's little village—they established congregations in several states.

The Missouri Synod launched a blistering attack on the
little synod soon after its founding, charging that it had a
weak grip on the Lutheran confessions. In particular, Iowa
was accused of errors in the doctrine of the church, its understanding of the ministry, and its teaching concerning the
last things. In response, the theologians of Iowa explained
that they understood the Lutheran confessions in a historical
sense, that is, that they interpeted them in light of the historical situation in which they were written. Iowa also argued that the Lutheran confessions are not a complete system of theology and that they leave certain questions open
to discussion and interpretation. This, in turn, occasioned
raised eyebrows in the Ohio Synod and elsewhere.

But Iowa held its ground and grew. It was a part of
Loehe's legacy to a country he never saw.

Texas Synod

By 1850, a variety of schemes for planting colonies in Texas had landed as many as 10,000 Germans there. Among the 10,000 there was only one Lutheran pastor, Caspar Braun, who had come from Pennsylvania. Braun organized a congregation in Houston and served it for 30 years.

Letters went to Europe telling of the crying need. News of the destitute Germans in Texas reached Switzerland and Christian Friedrich Spittler. He was director of a school for the training of missionaries at the Pilgrim's Mission of Saint Chrischona in a small Swiss village. When the situation in Texas came to Spittler's attention, he bent his energies to preparing missionaries for the struggling colonies. His school, supported by Christians of both Lutheran and Reformed churches, sent two pastors in 1850. The next year Saint Chrischona's entire class of six went to Texas.

By November of 1851, the Lutherans of Texas were ready to organize a synod. Seven pastors and one candidate for ordination met for three days and drew up a constitution for the "First Evangelical Lutheran Synod in Texas." Although never large, the synod took firm root among the German-American Lutherans of Texas. It helped that perhaps as many as 80 more pastors came from Saint Chrischona.

But even more were needed. The Texans looked first to the General Synod for help in securing pastors and then, in 1868, to the General Council. Unhappy in its connection with the Council, it later turned to the Iowa Synod and became a "district synod" of that larger body, although it retained some of the prerogatives of an independent body. On the southern border of the republic and absorbed in its tasks, the Texas Synod was relatively untouched by the controversies that periodically fired its larger counterparts. In questions of Lutheran unity it followed the lead of Iowa.

Norwegians

In hungry times, Norway's daughters and sons left for the United States. Beginning in 1825 and for a hundred years after that, they spilled out of its beautiful fjords in huge numbers. Like the Swedes, almost all of the Norwegians were Lutherans.

The first denomination among Norwegian-Americans was built by a lay preacher, Elling Eielsen. A firebrand Haugean from west Norway with piercing eyes and a scorching tongue, Eielsen gathered groups of awakened Norwegians into congregations, and in 1846 organized the congregations into the Evangelical Lutheran Church in America. "Eielsen's Synod," as the Norwegians called it, was a frontier version of the Haugean network in Norway. Its people practiced a religion of the heart. They demanded evidence of conversion from Christian believers and were quick to denounce what they thought of as the stone-cold Christianity of others.

Eielsen's Synod splintered several times. In 1876 a majority of Eielsen's Synod withdrew to reorganize as a more conventional denomination called Hauge's Evangelical Lutheran Synod in America. "Old Elling," as they called him, remained with his own small synod until he died in 1883.

The Haugeans were not long without denominational competitors on the Norwegian-American scene. In 1853 a group of lay delegates and young pastors met to form the Norwegian Evangelical Lutheran Church or "Norwegian Synod." The clergy of this church were a phalanx of formidable figures trained by the theological faculty of Norway's university. They were skilled theologians, excellent administrators, and passionate controversialists. A description of one of them would have fit them all. They were "orthodox to the fingertips."[6] They would sit on hard benches in cold churches and argue theology for hours to insure the doctrinal purity of their church. Their aim was to build a church confessional in every particular, and it was natural for them to strike early alliances with the Missouri Synod. The Missourians were quick to lend the Norwegian Synod aid, even training its pastors for a time.

The Haugeans stood at one end of the Norwegian-American spectrum and the Norwegian Synod at the other. It would not be long before people looked for a middle ground. Two new denominations emerged in 1870, when some Norwegians withdrew from their friendly cooperation with Swedish Lutherans in the Scandinavian Augustana Synod. One of these groups became the Norwegian Augustana Synod. This little synod survived for about 20 years and played a minor role in events to come. The other group to emerge out of this rearrangement was The Conference for the Norwegian-Danish Evangelical Lutheran Church. Deliberately setting out to claim the middle ground, the leaders of the Conference worked to build a church free of the presumptive piety they feared among the Haugeans and the authoritarian theology and practice they thought they detected in the Norwegian Synod.

Early on, a division of opinion created factions in the Conference. On one side, adherents of the "New School" suspected some of their colleagues of having minds in the mold of the Norwegian Synod. Members of the New School were concerned to make the congregation—"the free and living congregation," they liked to call it—the center of church life. They were suspicious of synods. The friends of the New School were also attached to the cause of Augsburg College and Seminary which, under the leadership of the brilliant Georg Sverdrup, came to embody their cause. Partisans of the "Old School" were concerned about what they thought of as a lack of interest in doctrine in the New School; they worried about its unwillingness to see the church elsewhere than in the congregation; and they did not share an allegiance to Augsburg.

While the Old and New Schools were squaring off in the Conference, yet another Norwegian-American group appeared on the scene. It appeared as one result of a controversy between the Missouri and Ohio Synods over the difficult theological notion of election to salvation. (More about this argument shortly.) Because of the Norwegian Synod's intimate relations with Missouri, its people were drawn into the controversy and divided by it. After a bitter battle, a large group of the Norwegian Synod's congregations and pastors withdrew from the Synod to form the Anti-Missourian Brotherhood, a coalition that set its sights on uniting as many other Norwegian-American Lutherans as possible. The Anti-Missourians made Saint Olaf's School, an academy in Minnesota that became a college, into their informal headquarters and trained their pastors there.

By the end of the 1880s, then, three groups stood poised between the Haugeans and the Norwegian Synod. They were the Norwegian-Augustana Synod, the Conference, and the Anti-Missourian Brotherhood. Despite the tensions within the groups and between them, capable leaders undertook delicate negotiations to bring them together, and in 1890 they suceeded. That year saw the United Norwegian Lutheran Church come into existence on a hot summer day at a celebrative convention in Minneapolis. The United Church was by name and definition a church built to include rather than exclude. Its leaders were early to urge Norwegian-Americans to come to terms with American culture for the sake of the church's mission.

The United Church did not enjoy peace for long. The new church had asked Augsburg to serve as its seminary and Saint Olaf to be its college. Partisans of the New School regarded this as an assault on the future of Augsburg and a threat to their theological convictions. After an extended struggle between the two factions—it included theological arguments, strident exchanges in conventions, court battles, and a lockout—they parted ways. It was another of those classic episodes involving ideas, people, and institutions in a scrap over the faith.

The New School's "Friends of Augsburg" went on to organize the Lutheran Free Church (LFC) in 1897. Augsburg College and Seminary were at the center of denominational life, and Georg Sverdrup became the mentor of the Free Church. Although it conceived of itself as more association than denomination, the Lutheran Free Church was forced by circumstances to take on denominational tasks. Its "Fundamental Principles and Rules for Work" guaranteed the autonomy of the local congregation and made it possible for any member of any congregation to vote in the conference of the church. A minimal polity and a lively piety—a Haugeanism unafraid of revival and fitted to American circumstances—powered the congregations of the LFC and gave it a character of its own among the Norwegian-American denominations.

By 1897, four sizable denominations had grown up among Norwegian-American Lutherans: Hauge's Synod, the Norwegian Synod, the United Church, and the Lutheran Free Church. They were still contending over awakening and confession, old antagonisms lingered yet, and hard fights were ahead, but a desire for unity was working like yeast among the Norwegians.

Danes

The "Sad" or "Holy" Danes who came to the United States were not sad, but earnest. They gained their name

DANISH LUTHERANS IN THE UNITED STATES

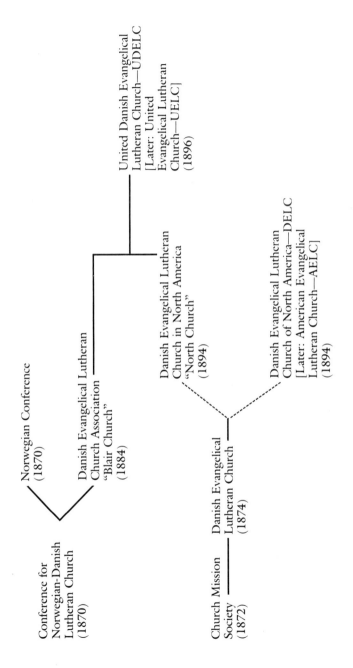

Conference for
Norwegian-Danish
Lutheran Church
(1870)

Norwegian Conference
(1870)

Danish Evangelical Lutheran
Church Association
"Blair Church"
(1884)

United Danish Evangelical
Lutheran Church—UDELC
[Later: United
Evangelical Lutheran
Church—UELC]
(1896)

Church Mission
Society
(1872) —— Danish Evangelical
Lutheran Church
(1874)

Danish Evangelical Lutheran
Church in North America
"North Church"
(1894)

Danish Evangelical Lutheran
Church of North America—DELC
[Later: American Evangelical
Lutheran Church—AELC]
(1894)

by their devotion to the preaching of repentance and salvation.

About the same time N. F. S. Grundtvig was giving shape to the traditions inherited by the "Happy" Danes, another kind of revival was also making itself felt. Under the powerful leadership of Pastor Vilhelm Beck, a Church Society for Inner Mission had been organized in 1861 to revive and awaken the Church of Denmark. Its work bore fruit as revivals spread in the congregations of the Danish church. The preachers of the Inner Mission—both lay people and pastors—called for repentance, a parting of ways with the world, and an active laity. The demand of the Inner Mission folk for repentance and moral rigor, the emphasis on the need for a "break" from the world, brought them the unfair name of "Sad" Danes.

The Danish pastors who came to the United States brought with them the traditions of either the "Happy" or the "Sad" Danes. The earliest to arrive cooperated with Norwegians in establishing the Conference for the Norwegian Danish Lutheran Church in 1870. Another group with pronounced Grundtvigian sympathies formed the Church Mission Society in 1872, which later became the Danish Evangelical Lutheran Church. When the Norwegians and Danes of the first group came to a friendly parting of ways, the Danes took steps toward creating a denomination of their own. In 1884, they organized the Danish Evangelical Lutheran Church Association in America. It was often called the "Blair Church" because it had its headquarters in the Nebraska town of that name. Most of its pastors were in sympathy with the Inner Mission and its methods.

Meanwhile, tensions inherited from Denmark set the Danish Evangelical Lutheran Church quivering, and it split into Grundtvigian and Inner Mission factions. The most divisive arguments were about whether the Bible *was* the

Word of God or *contained* the Word of God. In 1894 the contention divided the church, with 22 pastors—mostly favoring the Inner Mission tradition and holding the conviction that the Bible *was* God's Word—breaking away to form the Danish Evangelical Lutheran Church in North America. They called this the "North Church."

Two years later, the Blair Church and the North Church joined to form the United Danish Evangelical Church in America (UDELC). The denomination later changed its name by dropping the term *Danish,* and becoming the United Evangelical Lutheran Church (UELC). It carried on its earnest business through congregations located across the country in areas of Danish settlement. Although it was never large, those who lived in its congregations were sustained by a profound piety and a vigorous engagement with the world from which they had learned to "break" in order to return to it with the gospel.

Zion built

By the end of the 19th century, the upper Midwest was swarming with Lutherans. They had planted congregation after congregation and built synod after synod. America had opened possibilities for experimenting with Lutheranism, and the Lutherans had seized the opportunity to explore the size and shape of their traditions in the new situation. Each group had built by its own vision, each with its own sense of how to balance awakening and confession.

As the century closed, the Lutherans knew that their pioneering days in the Midwest were coming to an end. One of them—a Norwegian—looked back and said: "What have we done? We have built a Lutheran Zion over here."[7]

Alliances and Union

Zion divided

Unity long evaded the Lutherans of the Midwest. With congregations planted and synods organized, opinion was divided over the definition of Zion. They argued over it, they fought for it, they experimented with it—but for decades they could not achieve unity.

Some eastern Lutherans hoped that the General Council would catalyze unity among the fractious Lutherans to the west. Several synods were present at the exploratory meeting that led to the formation of the Council, and another had responded by letter. A member of the Ohio Synod had preached the opening sermon, and another Ohioan had served as temporary president of the convention.

The midwesterners were not at ease in the company of the eastern Lutherans. By 1867 the Missouri and Norwegian Synods had withdrawn from the deliberations and Iowa had asked for a voice but declined the privilege of a vote. Ohio kept cautiously apart, concerned about the doctrinal position of the Council. Ohio questioned four points of doctrine in particular: chiliasm (a doctrine holding that Christ will rule for a thousand years at the end of time), altar fellowship between Lutherans and with other Christians, pulpit exchanges between Lutherans and with Christians of different confessions, and secret societies or lodges. Unsatisfied by responses from the Council, Ohio did not join, and other midwestern bodies withdrew. Iowa remained in a restless relation with the Council until 1917.

Synodical Conference

The failure of the General Council to command the confidence of the midwesterners left open the question of the right alliance for them. As early as the 1850s, the Missouri Synod had sponsored a series of free conferences that helped conservative Lutherans get acquainted. Even Iowa and Buffalo had both undertaken independent conversations with Missouri, although little came of these efforts to heal old wounds. On again and off again, Ohio and Missouri had courted for decades. In 1868 the two synods held a brief meeting and announced that they were in complete agreement with each other.

It was not surprising, then, when Missouri responded happily to an invitation from Ohio to consider a new federation. Several other bodies—including the Norwegian Synod—accepted the invitation as well. In 1872 these synods created the Evangelical Lutheran Synodical Conference.

The Synodical Conference set its sights high. It aimed to unite all Lutheran synods on the basis of a common orthodoxy. "We will," one of its early leaders said,

> keep the treasure of the pure doctrine as our highest good and dearest jewel. This priceless treasure taken from the Word of God and set down in the doctrinal writings of our Lutheran church we will keep as a whole and in every detail unchanged and unchangeable.[8]

To insure purity of doctrine, there would be discussion, discussion, and more discussion—always of doctrine. It was a risky gambit, but undertaken in the confidence that ". . . the fight for pure doctrine will be a blessed one if it is based on the saving of souls. It is truly worth being called loveless and quarrelsome for the sake of this struggle."[9] Devotion to pure doctrine was the glue that kept these synods—different in so many ways—stuck together.

Election: grace *and* faith

The desire for theological unanimity made controversy inevitable.

Sparks struck tinder when the leading theologian of the Missouri Synod, C. F. W. Walther, discussed the difficult theological idea of election to salvation at a district convention in 1877. Other theologians suspected that Walther was making the salvation of believers into a mechanical fatalism. Opponents spoke up in Missouri, Ohio, and the Norwegian Synod.

All Lutherans insist that God alone saves, that he "elects" believers to salvation. But when it comes to finding a way to fit God's grace and human faith together, things get complicated. The Lutherans of the 19th century saw two alternatives. You could simply say that God in his good pleasure chooses to save those whom he will. Or, you could say that God chooses to save those whom he will in view of the faith he knows they will one day have. These two alternatives were called the "first form" and the "second form." Walther and most of his colleagues in Missouri were "first formers." Their opponents in Ohio and the other synods were "second formers." Both sides claimed the backing of the Lutheran confessions and the support of the Lutheran tradition.

It was a quarrel caused by the colliding claims of confession and experience. How can the confession of God's grace be maintained and—at the same time—the experience of faith be honored? What happens to faith if salvation is by grace alone? And what happens to grace if salvation is by faith alone? It is hard to answer both questions at once.

The parties to the argument in the 19th century never satisfied each other. In the end, Ohio and the Norwegian Synod withdrew from the Conference. The controversy left deep wounds, and its effects are felt to the present.

Norwegians unite

The Norwegian Synod was internally divided by the election controversy. The division was a bitter one marked by the word *split* in the histories of many congregations. After the defection of the Anti-Missourians, the Lutherans of the Norwegian Synod remained heavily behind the first form, while most other Norwegians inclined to the second form. Controversy had hardened the division of opinion.

In spite of the lingering tension, the United Church pressed for unity among the Norwegians. Leaders of the United Church were not discouraged in their efforts when a small group departed from their fold in 1900 to become the Church of the Lutheran Brethren. But the efforts of the United Church to further the cause of unity met little success until an initiative from Hauge's Synod finally prompted action. Memories of the election controversy and even older battles prevented reconciliation and progress until 1911. In that year two of the Norwegian churches adopted the tactic of appointing new committees composed of parish pastors rather than professional theologians. In 1912 the joint committees put the question of election into the hands of two pastors, locked them in a room, and told them not to come out until they could "thrash this thing out."[10] They came out with an agreement. They called it an *Opgjør,* or "Settlement."[11] The settlement amounted to an agreement to recognize both the first and second forms of election as appropriate Lutheran expressions for the reality of election

NORWEGIAN-AMERICAN LUTHERANISM, 1851–1917

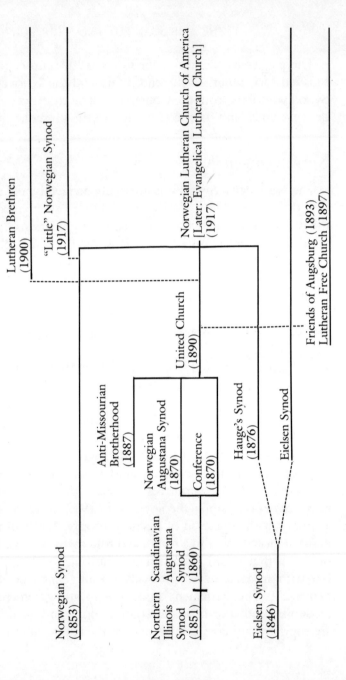

to salvation. In practical terms, the *Opgjør* was an agreement to disagree.

Missouri scorned the *Opgjør* as a hopeless compromise, but bells were rung in Norwegian congregations when news of the settlement was announced. The *Opgjør* made it possible for the three Norwegian denominations to move forward to a union in 1917. In that year the Norwegian Lutheran Church of America—composed of the Norwegian Synod, the United Church, and Hauge's Synod—began its life at a convention in Minneapolis. A small minority of the Norwegian Synod refused to enter the union and emerged as the Norwegian Synod of the American Evangelical Lutheran Church, often called the "Little" Norwegian Synod.

The old arguments never died, but the church seemed to thrive on them. The power of awakening and confession worked to keep the rambunctious Norwegians in endless ferment. They carried theological tensions and hearty pieties far into the 20th century. As they traveled into the future, they turned their skill at multiplying synods into an ability to multiply congregations that helped their church grow much larger than the other Scandinavian-American Lutheran churches.

The "Old" ALC

While the Norwegians were fighting their way toward unity, midwestern Germans tried to patch up old quarrels. The *Opgjør* permanently alienated the Norwegians and the Missouri Synod, but some pastors hoped that the Germans could settle the old election fight among themselves. Meetings were called and theses were written, but the old breaches could not be closed. The election controversy slid into oblivion, but it was never settled. Missouri remained adamant in its position and the other synods in theirs. The Norwegians made it plain that they would not be party to opening the question again.

When Iowa ended its tenuous connection with the General Council in 1917, it eased the suspicions Ohioans had of Iowans. The two synods had been working toward mutual understanding, and relations had been improving. With the stumbling block of membership in the General Council removed from the scene, it seemed to some that the time was ripe for Missouri's opponents to consider a union. Agitation for unity rose in Iowa and Ohio, and the two synods began negotiations. Committees declared the way open in 1922, and a merger commission started work. In 1925 the Buffalo Synod asked to be included in the negotiations. Texas had been along from the beginning through its connection with Iowa.

Hopes for quick action were blasted when a new doctrinal controversy erupted. When a constitution for the new church was drafted, a statement on the Scripture described it as "inerrant." J. M. Reu, Iowa's premier theologian, rose up to demand removal of the word. He insisted that the mode of Scripture's inspiration belonged to the category of "open questions" for which Iowa had shed so much blood in its wars with Missouri. A battle in and between the two synods followed. It took a compromise to make the union possible. The term *infallible* was used of the Scripture in the doctrinal article of the new constitution and the word *inerrant* was included in an appendix to the constitution.[12] With the inspiration controversy settled, the four synods entered into the American Lutheran Church in 1930. Because another church would assume an almost identical name in 1960, the ALC of 1930 is often remembered as the "Old" ALC.

Early and late in the life of the ALC of 1930 there was

talk of a mission to build bridges between synods. It proved a mission impossible to fulfill. Conversations and agreements with both the ULCA and Missouri failed to produce fellowship. Debate over the inspiration and inerrancy of Scripture obstructed progress with the ULCA, and uniformity in doctrine and practice was the stumbling block with Missouri.

The ALC did not succeed in raising the bridges it dreamed of building. It had, though, brought German-American Lutherans of several synods together. And it did keep the kettle stirred. In its life of 30 years, it insisted that its synodical neighbors ponder the definition of Lutheran unity.

A crucial decade

The 1920s were a worrisome time for American Christians. They were ashamed of their chauvinistic excesses during World War I, depressed over the dangerous uselessness of the war, and much given to talk of pacifism. Socialist agitation and labor unrest disturbed the status quo. Moral crusades to right the wrongs of the world abounded, while other people wondered about what looked like new kinds of immorality. Older folks who remembered simpler days sat on front porches and worried about their children and the dangers of flivvers and flappers.

While the 20s roared, American Protestantism was beginning to divide down the middle. On one hand, some individuals and churches gravitated toward a theology adjusted to the new findings of scientists and historians, an optimistic social activism prompted by changing conditions in American life, and an ecumenism oriented to cooperation in practice rather than the definition of the faith. These Christians inherited the liberal tradition of American religion and were sometimes called Modernists. Ranged against them were a loose coalition of Protestants, the Fundamentalists. The Fundamentalists defended a variety of conservative theologies, advocated moral codes largely directed to the individual rather than society, and were cautious about cooperation among Christians who did not agree on doctrine. Defense of the Bible was their common cause. They staked their case on the inspiration and inerrancy of Scripture.

Modernists and Fundamentalists had been exchanging fire for years when their battle suddenly became a contest of champions. In the summer of 1925 Clarence Darrow and William Jennings Bryan tilted at the "Monkey Trial" in Dayton, Tennessee over the teaching of evolution in public schools. Bryan, the advocate of conservative Protestantism, won the case at law, but seems to have lost it in the court of public opinion. All the ballyhoo of his boosters backfired, and conservative Christianity appeared to be in retreat.

Midwestern Lutherans watched all this and fretted. It seemed as if the old ills of Europe had infected America. Socialism, Darwinism, historical criticism of the Scripture, and an ecumenism they regarded as illegitimate—"unionism," they called it—had come knocking at their backdoor.

American Lutheran Conference

In retrospect it is not surprising that German synods of the Midwest were agitated by a controversy over inerrancy on their way to forming the American Lutheran Church of 1930. The Lutherans of the midwestern bodies were united in their suspicion of Modernism and allied in sympathy with the Fundamentalists.

The Lutherans took quick action to lock arms. Even before the organization of the National Lutheran Council, representatives of midwestern synods had considered a new federation.[13] In 1925 a conference was arranged between representatives of the Norwegian Lutheran Church, the

THE AMERICAN LUTHERAN CHURCH 89

Ohio Synod, and the Iowa Synod. At the meeting in Minneapolis, discussion began with the Chicago Theses that H. G. Stub of the Norwegians had prepared in 1919 for talks in the National Lutheran Council. In light of the times, Stub again insisted on including the term *inerrant* to describe the Holy Scriptures. When discussions revealed agreement on other disputed issues, a new set of theses were prepared and named after the city in which the meeting had been held.[14]

The Minneapolis Theses became the doctrinal platform of a new federation, the American Lutheran Conference, organized in 1930. The membership of the Conference included the American Lutheran Church (1930), the Augustana Synod, the Norwegian Lutheran Church of America, the Lutheran Free Church, and the United Danish Evangelical Lutheran Church. These bodies were all members of the National Lutheran Council as well.

The American Lutheran Conference was a natural partnership. Largely second- and third-generation immigrants living in the upper Mississippi Valley, the people of these churches had much in common. At the same time, the new federation was a defensive alliance. The churches of the American Lutheran Conference all shared a history of affection and antagonism toward the Missouri Synod and all of them were suspicious of theological liberalism (especially with respect to the doctrine of Scripture) in the ULCA. Their common background made mutual effort natural, but not always easy. There was the predictable impulse to defend ecclesiastical turf, aggravated by ethnic loyalties and sometimes overlapping home mission efforts. In an exasperated moment, a veteran leader of the Conference called this competition a "ring around the rosy" of denominational anxieties.[15] But in the end these Lutherans came to know and trust each other.

FORMING THE ALC, 1900-1963

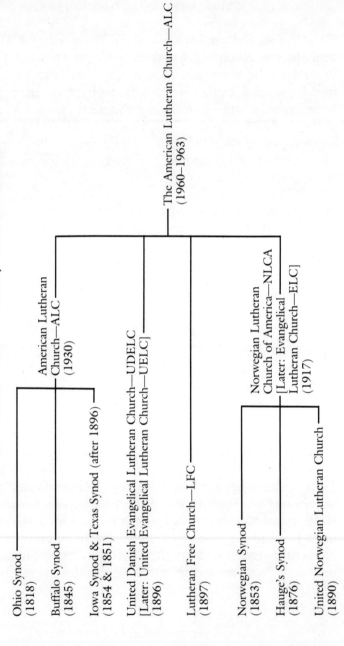

Ohio Synod
(1818)

Buffalo Synod
(1845)

Iowa Synod & Texas Synod (after 1896)
(1854 & 1851)

American Lutheran
Church—ALC
(1930)

United Danish Evangelical Lutheran Church—UDELC
[Later: United Evangelical Lutheran Church—UELC]
(1896)

Lutheran Free Church—LFC
(1897)

Norwegian Synod
(1853)

Norwegian Lutheran
Church of America—NLCA
[Later: Evangelical
Lutheran Church—ELC]
(1917)

Hauge's Synod
(1876)

United Norwegian Lutheran Church
(1890)

The American Lutheran Church—ALC
(1960–1963)

Union

During World War II, intensive cooperation between Lutherans prompted proposals in the interests of Lutheran unity. One proposal called for a federation of the bodies belonging to the National Lutheran Council. Another suggested enlarging the American Lutheran Conference. A third revived the old idea of the "free conference" for the sake of discussion (and the conscience of Missourians who thought this the only appropriate course).

In 1948 and 1949, Augustana and the ULCA backed proposals for merger or a federation of the National Lutheran Council. The Danish UELC and the Evangelical Lutheran Church or ELC (as the Norwegian Lutheran Church had been renamed) countered by collaborating in actions calling for the merger of their two churches and at least one other body of the American Lutheran Conference.

When efforts to federate or unite the churches of the National Lutheran Council collapsed, the possibility remained that the churches of the American Lutheran Conference might merge. In 1952 a Joint Union Committee of the Conference bodies presented a statement, *The United Testimony,* to the churches.[16] Although not in the form of theses, it continued the characteristic midwestern pattern of attempting to express agreement on disputed issues. It therefore covered a variety of questions, both practical and theological. In its discussion of the Bible it affirmed the historical character of the Scriptures and at the same time called it "inerrant."[17] This juxtaposition reflected differing theological positions. Affirmation of the historical nature of the Bible came from Augustana, and the statement on inerrancy was included at the insistence of its partner churches, especially the ELC.

Despite its willingness to collaborate in the writing of *The*

Georg Sverdrup
1848–1907

Hans Gerhard Stub
1849–1931

The three church body presidents at the time of the merger that formed the ALC were (l. to r.) Fredrik A. Schiotz (b. 1901) of the Evangelical Lutheran Church, William Larsen (1909–1971) of the United Evangelical Lutheran Church, and Henry F. Schuh (1890–1965) of the American Lutheran Church. In 1962 the Lutheran Free Church became part of the ALC; the president of the LFC at that time was John Stensvaag (b. 1911).

United Testimony, the Augustana Church (it had changed its name from "Synod" to "Church") withdrew from preparations for the merger of the American Lutheran Conference. The first preference of many of Augustana's leaders had been for a merger of the churches of the National Lutheran Council, and Augustana's participation in merger talks in the American Lutheran Conference had been conditional from the beginning. When time came for a decision, Augustana explained that it was unwilling to enter a union not open to all Lutheran bodies and in which the question of ecumenical relations was not high on the working agenda. Behind these reasons were the facts of Augustana's long history of friendship with the eastern Lutherans of the General Council and the ULCA, a different theological outlook in evidence since changes in Augustana's theological faculty in 1930, and a competitive spirit that occasionally surfaced between the Swedish and Norwegian churches and their aggressive leaders. The parting made a hard moment for friends.

Augustana, the ULCA, and two other bodies went forward toward the merger creating the LCA in 1962.

The remaining four bodies of the American Lutheran Conference continued preparations for a merger. They retained *The United Testimony* as a platform, but when a constitution for the emerging body was prepared, its ambiguous position on Scripture was altered. In the constitution of the new church, the Holy Scriptures were declared "inerrant" without qualification.[18]

With disputed questions apparently resolved, the American Lutheran Church, the Evangelical Lutheran Church, and the United Evangelical Lutheran Church united in 1960 to create the new American Lutheran Church. After proposals to enter the union were twice defeated, a third referendum brought the Lutheran Free Church into the new

American Lutheran Church in 1963. Congregations of the Free Church not wishing to enter the merged church withdrew to form the small Association of Free Lutheran Congregations.

What does it mean to be Lutheran in America?

How did the new American Lutheran Church answer this old question?

The traditions contributing to the ALC first came to the United States with immigrants from Denmark, the German lands, and Norway. Most of these immigrants had come in the great rivers of people that poured in between 1850 and 1925. By the middle of the 20th century the descendants of the immigrants were comfortably at home in the United States. An ethnic veneer was sometimes apparent, but it was thin. Few spoke the old languages, and many a Lutheran from the Midwest who traveled to Europe was surprised to learn how much distance there was between the European and American versions of Lutheranism.

Most of the leaders who built the ALC were steeped in the conservative theology of 19th-century Lutheran confessionalism. They understood agreement or explicit agreement to disagree in doctrine to be a fundamental element of Lutheran unity. To a European tradition of emphasizing the inspiration and authority of Scripture, they added the American Fundamentalist insistence on use of the term *inerrant* to describe the Scriptures. Their traditions made them exceedingly cautious about ecumenical relations beyond the Lutheran household.

But the makers of its merger did not have the last word on doctrine in the ALC. Changing winds were blowing through the seminaries of the merging churches even before they united. Theologians were introducing new ideas from both European and American sources. Inerrancy was widely rejected by the theologians, and historical criticism of the Scriptures broadly endorsed. The Lutheran confessions were interpreted historically and critically. Theological variety was the order of the day. Like their counterparts in the LCA, the theologians of the new ALC entered into the sometimes bewildering diversity of theology in the 20th century. Turning from inherited Lutheran questions to a ceaselessly changing agenda, they more often spoke of options than answers.

By 1960 the churches had also entered deeply into the ecumenical movement in its local, national, and global dimensions. A vigorous debate in the ELC prior to merger saw a proposal to join the World Council of Churches first defeated and then later passed by a considerable margin. It was an index of changing times in that large church, and the others were moving in new directions as well.

These theological and ecumenical developments meant that even before they merged, the churches on their way to becoming the new ALC were moving away from the doctrinal position that made their merger possible. Changes did not come painlessly, and it required considerable skill of its first president, Frederik A. Schiotz, and other leaders to reckon with the potential of conflict in the early years.

The liturgy of the Lord's Supper and the preaching service have a complexion much as elsewhere among American Lutherans. Traditions brought from Europe and once painstakingly observed in America—registering with the pastor before Communion, for example—have largely vanished. As in the LCA, a strong liturgical movement has made itself felt, but it is often balanced by the free spirit of inherited pieties. The old mix of awakening and confession is still brewing in the ALC. Inherited moral codes are followed in some families and congregations, but in others they are more often questioned than observed. Abstinence from alcohol as a religious practice, for example, is scarcer than it once was. The formerly divisive question of secret societies is little in evidence.

How does it make a church?

According to its constitution, the ALC ". . . accepts all the canonical books of the Old and New Testaments as a whole and in all their parts as the divinely inspired, revealed, and inerrant Word of God. . . ." The three ecumenical creeds, along with the *Augsburg Confession* and Luther's *Small Catechism*, are called "brief and true statements of the doctrines of the Word of God." The other Lutheran Confessions are received as elaborations of the two primary symbols. All congregations and members of the church are said by the constitution to subscribe to these confessions, ". . . not insofar as but because they are the presentation and explanation of the pure doctrine of the Word of God and a summary of the faith of the evangelical Lutheran Church."[19]

The ALC defines itself as a union of congregations, and a temperate congregationalism is a part of the spirit of the church. That definition and spirit reflect the early history of its traditions. Congregations preceded pastors in the polity and early experience of the antecedent bodies, and to this day congregations guard their autonomy carefully. The term *ministerium* is rarely used in the ALC, and the clergy do not constitute an independent element in the definition of the church. Pastors do not vote in district conventions unless they serve or represent congregations.

The ALC includes almost 5000 congregations, with close to two and a half million baptized members.[20] The people

of the ALC live across the country but are heavily concentrated in the upper Midwest, where wags like to say Lutherans are dense.

The districts of the ALC are large—there are only 19 of
them—and there is often a considerable sense of distance
between congregations and their districts. District conventions are, however, held annually and district presidents or
their assistants are regularly involved in the calling of pastors. In recent years, district presidents (like synod presidents in the LCA) have been called bishops, and there has
been agitation for them to take on a more pastoral role in
the affairs of the congregations. Districts have also been
called upon to take up more responsibility in developing
programs for congregations.

Like its large Protestant counterparts, the ALC models
its national structure on the plan of a corporation. It is built
of boards, executives, and staffs answerable to the church
through general conventions.

Although they have built a bureaucracy of several layers
for their church, the people of the ALC are often hesitant
to rely on structure to order its work. It is sometimes said
that the ALC works more as if it were a big family than a
large denomination. This is more nostalgic than accurate,
but there is a grain of truth to it. The familial feel of the
smaller churches is gone, but a hesitance about structure
and bureaucracy remains. On the other hand, there still ex-
ists in the ALC a tradition of confidence in authoritative
(and even authoritarian) personal leadership. Congregations, districts, boards, and the national church have now
and then chafed, but usually responded, to the direction of
able leaders.

How has the ALC answered the question, What does it
mean to be Lutheran in America? Its builders tried to offer
a single answer to the question. With European traditions

of confession and awakening behind them, the people of these churches moved toward each other in the confidence that the authority of Scripture, the testimony of their confessions, the pursuit of doctrinal theology, and the experience of living faith could unite them in building a Lutheran Zion in America. Through the middle of the 20th century, they struggled to unite on a definition of Lutheran identity. When at last they came to agreement, young leaders stood ready to experiment with new questions and new answers. They went to work in a church lively with old traditions of awakening and confession.

THE ASSOCIATION OF EVANGELICAL LUTHERAN CHURCHES

1976

Uniting

The Association of Evangelical Lutheran Churches is the smallest and newest of the three American Lutheran churches talking about uniting in the 1980s. Its roots are in the Missouri Synod.

What is now called the Lutheran Church–Missouri Synod was organized as "The German Evangelical Lutheran Synod of Missouri, Ohio, and Other States" at a series of meetings in 1846 and 1847. Its sturdy name tells some of its early history.

Loehe's Lutherans

F. C. D. Wyneken, the young German missionary of the Pennsylvania Ministerium who had arrived in the United States in 1838 and whose plea on behalf of the Lutherans in America caught the eye of Pastor Wilhelm Loehe in Neuendettelsau, returned to Germany for a visit in 1841. Wyneken encouraged Loehe's interest in America and asked him to train missionaries for the new country. Before long, missionaries sent by Loehe were scattered through several synods and encamped in frontier settlements where they hoped to establish schools and evangelize Native Americans.

Several of Loehe's missionaries who had affiliated with existing synods quickly found themselves restless. Trained in the conservative confessionalism of the Neuendettelsau pastor, they thought doctrine and practice in the American synods lax. Wyneken himself had not been taught by Loehe, but his experience of religion on the American frontier had turned him into a rigorous confessionalist. Like the missionaries sent by Loehe, he looked for a synodical home congenial to his brand of Lutheranism. He would find friendly company when he made contact with other newly arrived Lutherans from Germany, a colony of Saxons in Missouri.

Saxons

The same year Wyneken came to America, a group of Lutherans in the Saxon city of Dresden were preparing to migrate to the United States.

Like other awakened Lutherans, they were uneasy in the Saxon church. They had gathered around Pastor Martin Stephan, who had been pastor of the Saint John congregation in Dresden since 1810. The young were especially attracted to this stirring preacher, and under his ministry the membership of his congregation increased sixfold in 10 years. Stephan preached from texts of the Bible and brought home the message of justification by faith to his hearers.

Officials of the government and older members of the Saint John congregation were alarmed by what they regarded as Lutheran extremism and took action to contain Stephan. He was harassed, put under surveillance, and jailed on charges of immorality. As pressure from the authorities increased, the group around Stephan talked of going to America. Eventually about 700 Saxons boarded five ships sailing for America in the winter of 1838. At sea, those who sailed with Stephan on the ship *Olbers* invested him with the title of bishop and granted him extraordinary power over the affairs of the colony in the making.

By the time the four ships surviving the Atlantic crossing had landed and the colonists had made their way up the Mississippi to Saint Louis, Stephan had emerged as autocrat of the Saxons. When most of the colony moved to land purchased in nearby Perry County, Stephan remained installed in the best quarters available in Saint Louis. The colonists went to work clearing and building at his direction, while a small party of Saxons remained in Saint Louis with Stephan. Three of them were his undoing. When Stephan was away on a visit to Perry County, two young women confessed to elders of the church of having had improper relations with Stephan. A third woman reported advances she had rebuffed. One of the pastors living in Saint Louis, C. F. W. Walther, made public the accusations against Stephan and forced a showdown. Stephan was evicted from the colony and sent to an exile in Illinois.

C. F. W. Walther

The community was stunned. Were they still the church? They had cut their ties to the Saxon church at home. Stephan had betrayed their trust. To whom could they turn?

The pastor from Saint Louis, C. F. W. Walther, emerged as the new leader of the Saxons. An erudite student of Luther

Martin Stephan
1777–1846

C. F. W. Walther
1811–1887

and the Lutheran scholastics, Walther developed a theology of the church designed to help the bewildered Germans understand their new situation. A public debate was arranged for Walther to argue that the Word of God at work among believers gathers them into congregations, that the Word and people together make the church. The church— and this must have instantly persuaded most of the disappointed Saxons—does not depend for its existence on bishops or ordained clergy. The church makes itself known in the congregations of believers gathered around the Word spoken in the sermon and active in the sacraments.

Walther carried the day. The colony recovered its morale. Fields were plowed, churches were raised, schools were opened. By 1844, the community was strong enough to support the publication of a newspaper, and Walther became its editor. The first issue of *Der Lutheraner*—"The Lutheran"—appeared in September of that year. *Der Lutheraner* sent the sound of Walther's powerful voice far and wide. It took the message of Missouri's mission with it.

Founding the Synod

When F. C. D. Wyneken read the first issue of *Der Lutheraner*, he knew he had found the sisters and brothers in faith for whom he had been looking. He is said to have exclaimed, "Thank God there are other true Lutherans in America!"

At home in Neuendettelsau, Loehe had been following events in America. He wrote to ask if it were not time for the conservative Germans to think of establishing their own synod. Loehe's question was passed on to Walther, who responded positively. Walther was also in contact with some of Loehe's pastors in Ohio. Several meetings between emissaries of both groups resulted in decisions to form a new synod dedicated to the causes of conservative German Lutheranism in the United States.

The lessons the Saxons had learned in Perry County helped them build their new synod. The congregation was regarded as the essential manifestation of the church. The ministerial office was thought of as "transferred" to pastors by the baptized believers of congregations. The synod was built as an advisory body to assist the congregations in matters of mutual concern. Doctrinal supervision was vested in the synod, but it was given no coercive power over the congregations. The synod's doctrinal position was expressed in two specific provisions of its constitution.

Under the statement, "Synod, and every member of Synod, accepts without reservation . . ." were these two articles:

1. The Scriptures of the Old and the New Testament as the written Word of God and the only rule and norm of faith and of practice.

2. All the Symbolical Books of the Evangelical Lutheran Church as a true and unadulterated statement and exposition of the Word of God, to wit, the three Ecumenical Creeds (the Apostles' Creed, the Nicene Creed, the Athanasian Creed), the Unaltered Augsburg Confession, the Apology of the Augsburg Confession, the Smalcald Articles, the Large Catechism of Luther, the Small Catechism of Luther, and the Formula of Concord.[1]

A green bough from the old oak

As the new synod grew, an eastern Lutheran looked to the West and said,

This Lutheranism of the old unaltered confession of ancient forms has sprouted like a green bough from the old oak, and has been thriving during the last few years in our midst. It stands by itself, but it also grows by itself.[2]

The new synod did grow quickly. The phrase "in Other States" was entered into its name as a descriptive phrase, but it might also have been taken as a promise. Decade after decade, the synod spread itself across the country.

Walther and his colleagues aimed to create a German Lutheran culture sealed against the spirit and forms of American Protestantism. They hoped to create a safe sphere for the cultivation of pure doctrine, the practice of faithful worship, and the pursuit of learning and the arts. They counted on the German language as a first barrier against foreign invasion, but relied on pure doctrine as their inner line of defense. They intended their doctrinal fortifications to hold even when the children began to speak English. *Lehre* or "doctrine" was often spoken of as *Wehre* or "defense."

To guarantee the cultivation of German and the preservation of the pure doctrine, the founders of the synod published carefully chosen literature and built a complete school system. Walther hoped to establish a German university, but did not see his hopes fulfilled. He did, however, witness the founding of schools intended to meet all the practical needs of the synod. For several generations most of its pastors received all of their education in the parochial schools, colleges, and seminaries of the synod. This pedagogical enclosure produced an extraordinary homogeneity in the synod. Inculcated in its pastors and laity was a sense of "Synod"—always without the definite article—as a living entity. A high premium was placed on consensus.

Missouri looked for the same homogeneity in the Synodical Conference it helped create in 1872. It was an essay by Walther that provoked the election controversy that disrupted the Conference in the 1880s, and in that fight Walther's intransigence and Missouri's insistence on uniformity in doctrine and practice were among the factors that led the Ohio and Norwegian Synods to withdraw. The Conference never fully recovered from the controversy, and when it was over Missouri stood increasingly alone. Alone, but vital as a green shoot from an old oak.

Franz Pieper

When Walther died in 1875, an Elisha stood ready to take on the mantle of Elijah. Franz Pieper became the guardian of Missouri's theology.

Two theological landmarks in the history of the Missouri Synod were produced by Pieper. One is his large *Christian Dogmatics*,[3] from which generations of Missouri's pastors learned doctrinal theology, and the other is a document written largely by Pieper and approved by the synod in 1932, "A Brief Statement of the Doctrinal Position of the Evangelical Lutheran Synod of Missouri, Ohio, and Other States."[4] Although never elevated to confessional rank, this statement has had an authority almost like that of a confession in the deliberations of the synod. It was written as a summary of the synod's stand on issues over which it had been in controversy or thought likely to be controversial.

At work in a period when historical criticism of Scripture was advancing on both European and American fronts, Pieper insisted on a conservative, 19th-century version of the doctrines of inspiration and infallibility. Here are passages from the beginning of "A Brief Statement:"

> We teach that the Holy Scriptures differ from all other books in the world in that they are the Word of God. They are the Word of God because the holy men of God who wrote the Scriptures wrote only that which the Holy Ghost communicated to them by inspiration. . . . Since the Holy Scriptures are the Word of God, it goes without saying that they contain no errors or contradictions, but that they are in all their parts and words the infallible truth, also in those parts which treat of historical, geographical, and other secular matters. . . .[5]

Under Pieper's tutoring, adherence to this notion of inspiration and infallibility (often spoken of as "inerrancy") became a litmus test of doctrinal purity in Missouri.

Cracks in the consensus

In spite of the authority of its mentors and its homogeneity, the consensus in Missouri began to weaken not long after Pieper died in 1931. By 1945 it was impossible to keep the cracks from public view. In that year 44 members of the synod signed and published "A Statement" of 12 positive affirmations, some followed by grave complaints against the synod. From a distance, the complaints reveal more about the situation in the synod than do the affirmations. For example:

> We deplore . . . any and every tendency which would limit the power of our heritage, reduce it to narrow legalism, and confine it by manmade traditions.

> We deplore . . . a tendency in our Synod to substitute human judgments, synodical resolutions, or other sources of authority for the supreme authority of Scripture.

> We deplore . . . any tendency which reduces the warmth and power of the Gospel to a set of intellectual propositions. . . .[6]

Even more significant than the action of the "Forty-four," as the signers of this statement came to be called, were changes to come in the synod's theological faculty at Saint Louis. By the end of the 1950s, historical criticism had arrived to stay for a while among the theologians of Missouri.

The "Forty-four" had been induced to "withdraw" their statement on procedural grounds, but what of the theologians who were teaching the seminarians of the church? In the 1960s a prominent associate of the president of the synod warned,

> We have not dealt honestly with our pastors and people. We have refused to state our changing theological position. . . . Over and over again we said nothing was changing, but all the while we were aware of changes taking place.[7]

In a church that placed a high premium on consensus, trouble was brewing.

The storm broke in 1969. After bilateral conversations between the ALC and Missouri and preliminary approval by a Missouri Synod convention, the synod's president recommended the establishment of fellowship between the ALC and Missouri. Fearing compromise of the synod's traditions, conservative forces marshaled opposition to the synod's leadership and succeeded in unseating the president in favor of a conservative candidate, J. A. O. Preus. Fellowship with the ALC was, however, approved in a sharply divided vote.

Dividing

Seminex

In the same year that J. A. O. Preus was elected president of the synod, a new president was named for Concordia Seminary in Saint Louis, John H. Tietjen. Tietjen brought experience in inter-Lutheran affairs to his new post and was expected to help lead the Missouri Synod into new ventures in cooperation with other Lutherans. He did not have the opportunity to fulfill those expectations. Within months of

Tietjen's arrival at Concordia, Preus announced the beginning of an investigation of affairs at the seminary.

In 1972 Preus issued a report severely critical of the seminary.[8] Tietjen countered with his own statement, taking issue with the synodical president's report in polemical language.[9] When the matter was put before the synod in convention, a majority of the delegates voted to censure the faculty for false doctrine. Key issues were the inspiration and inerrancy of Scripture and use of the historical critical method of biblical interpretation. Over these things, Missouri sensed itself divided between "conservatives" and "moderates."

Charges against Tietjen were referred to the board of Concordia Seminary. The seminary board, in the hands of conservatives, suspended the moderate Tietjen in January of 1974. Seminarians at Concordia rose in protest and declared a moratorium on classes. In support of Tietjen, the faculty refused to teach until cleared of the charge of false doctrine. On February 19, most of the faculty and students of the institution left the campus of Concordia Seminary to take up their work in quarters elsewhere. They formed Concordia Seminary in Exile, familiarly known as "Seminex."

ELIM and division

In 1973, the year before the disruptions at Concordia Seminary, moderates had organized Evangelical Lutherans in Mission (ELIM) in order to make their causes known and to effect change within the synod. In 1975, Missouri's synodical convention censured the activities of ELIM as "schismatic" and called on its members to abandon either ELIM or the Synod. Another potentially divisive question before the convention was what to do with graduates of Seminex. Could they be permitted to receive and accept calls

John H. Tietjen, b. 1928
President Concordia
Seminary, St. Louis
President "Seminex"

J. A. O. Preus, b. 1920
President LCMS

William H. Kohn, b. 1915
First president AELC

to the congregations of the Missouri Synod? District presidents were admonished not to ordain or place seminarians not authorized through the synod's regular procedures.

When four district presidents continued to ordain and place graduates of Seminex, they were removed from office by Preus in April of 1976. The action provoked dismay and reaction. In December of 1976 moderates took final steps to organize the Association of Evangelical Lutheran Churches (AELC). William H. Kohn served as first president of the new Association.

In 1977, statistics showed that Missouri had lost more than 86,000 members and 107 congregations.[10] Over two and one-half million members and more than 6000 congregations remained.[11] At present, the AELC has just under 300 congregations with a little more than 100,000 baptized members.

Exile

In its exile the AELC inherits traditions of nationality, chronology, and geography from Missouri. Its people are scattered across the country. Many of them are descended from German immigrants and many are not. A passion for mission has made Missouri—and so the AELC—home to a multitude of families not born to its traditions but converted to them.

In doctrine the AELC claims the legacy of Missouri. The doctrinal article in the constitution of the AELC is nearly identical to the corresponding statement in Missouri's constitution. The AELC's statement is different in its ringing first affirmation, "We joyfully acknowledge and confess without reservation . . ." and in its inclusion of the *Treatise on the Power and Primacy of the Pope* in the list of confessions subscribed.[12] The substance of the old statement was retained by the new AELC, as one of its theologians said, ". . . to express their conviction that they and not the advocates of binding doctrinal statements were the true representatives of the Missouri Synod's historical position."[13]

The claim that the AELC holds the historical position of Missouri calls for some qualification. The theologians of the AELC generally endorse the historical-critical method of biblical interpretation and display the same diversity as theologians in the ALC and LCA. They have often engaged with the contemporary ecumenical movement. Theologians, pastors, and congregations of the new church have put themselves in the thick of the movement toward Lutheran unity. Everywhere in the AELC women have taken their places as leaders of the churches. In these things the AELC has departed from the traditions of Missouri. But the old sense of identity and mission lingers. The people of the AELC sometimes think of themselves as a purified remnant of Missouri.

In public piety the people and congregations of the AELC show the same diversity and vitality as the Missouri Synod. As elsewhere in American Lutheranism, much liturgical renewal and experimentation is in evidence. Some congregations in the AELC have elaborated the catholic elements of Lutheran liturgical life to a high degree.

As in Missouri, the congregation is the central element in the polity of the AELC. Its congregations—some of them tried sorely by controversy and their decision to depart from Missouri—guard their autonomy carefully. They are gathered into regional synods and one nongeographical synod, the English Synod. The national assembly of the church meets every two years and is restricted to duties assigned to it by the synods. Unlike its parent body, the AELC is served by ordained women.

It was a bold venture for the women and men of the AELC to leave an old home in which most of them had grown up. Yet, like all of us who leave home, they took the long story of their family with them. They have been liberal in sharing it with friends.

AND NOW HOW MANY?

Three large churches and a smaller one? Two large churches? Is there hope of one Lutheran church in the United States? And what about unity beyond the American Lutheran household?

Stories from the long haul toward Lutheran unity will not answer the questions for us, but they can help us reckon with them. Historians are always annoying people with the adage that those who forget the past are condemned to repeat its mistakes. They would not say it so often if it were not true. The reminder might not be so irksome if the historians would think to add that those who do remember the past are allowed to pick up its possibilities and put them to use in the present.

The stories of our past warn us of how taxing the questions in front of us are, and they welcome us to the adventure of answering. Our stories have advice to give and suggestions to offer. And, like the members of any new generation, we have the opportunity of taking, leaving, and creating in response. It would be sad if we missed the opportunity to do that. That kind of thing is an important part of growing up in any family.

Our stories also issue a challenge. If there is one thing the people of our past ask of us, it is that we consider our *identity* when we think about our *unity*. "And now how many?" is not the only question on the table. It is also our turn to ask and answer the question, What does it mean to be Lutheran in America? Beyond that looms the even larger question of the proper place of American Lutherans in the whole of Christ's church.

God can be counted on to be as generous to us as he was to our forebears. If we can be as earnest as they were in asking and answering the important questions, our story will deserve a place next to theirs.

NOTES

Documents = Richard C. Wolf, *Documents of Lutheran Unity in America* (Philadelphia: Fortress Press, 1966).

Where possible, citations are to Wolf's collection. Those who wish to consult original sources may refer to Wolf's appendix, "Sources," for documentation.

All These Lutherans . . . All Those Synods

1. See John Higham, *Strangers in the Land: Patterns of American Nativism, 1860–1925,* 2nd ed. (New York: Atheneum, 1978), p. 248.
2. Quoted in Will Herberg, *Protestant—Catholic—Jew: An Essay in American Religious Sociology* (Garden City, New York: Doubleday & Company, 1955), p. 97.

The Lutheran Church in America·

1. Quoted in Richard C. Wolf, *Lutherans in North America* (Philadelphia: Lutheran Church Press, 1965), p. 2.
2. From a pamphlet by J. A. Walther, quoted in Carl Mauelshagen, *Salzburg Lutheran Expulsion and Its Impact* (New York: Vantage Press, 1962), p. 122.

3. Philip Jacob Spener, *Pia Desideria,* ed. and tr. Theodore G. Tappert, Seminar Editions (Philadelphia: Fortress Press, 1964).

4. See *The Journals of Henry Melchior Muhlenberg,* ed. and tr. Theodore G. Tappert and John W. Doberstein, vol. 3 (Philadelphia: The Evangelical Lutheran Ministerium of Pennsylvania and Adjacent States and the Muhlenberg Press, 1948), p. 67.

5. For the complete record of this first "convention," see *Documentary History of the Evangelical Lutheran Ministerium of Pennsylvania and Adjacent States* (Philadelphia: Board of Publication of the General Council of the Evangelical Lutheran Church in North America, 1898), pp. 3-23.

6. *Documentary History of the Evangelical Lutheran Ministerium of Pennsylvania and Adjacent States,* pp. 248-259.

7. *Evangelical Catechism: or a Short Exposition of the Principle Doctrines and Precepts of the Christian Religion, for the Use of the Churches Belonging to the Evangelical Lutheran Synod of State of New York* (Hudson: William & Norman, 1814).

8. "General Synod on Civil War, 1862," *Documents,* pp. 119-122.

9. Philadelphia: General Council Publication Board, 1871.

10. "Definite Synodical Platform, 1855," *Documents,* pp. 100-104.

11. "Krauth's Theses on Faith and Polity, 1866," *Documents,* pp. 143-148.

12. "Galesburg Rule, 1875," *Documents,* p. 171.

13. A *Common Service* was adopted by the General Synod, the General Council, and the United Synod, South in 1887. It was published in varying editions beginning in 1888. A hymnal was included in the *Common Service Book of the Lutheran Church* (Philadelphia and Columbia, S.C., 1917).

14. Respectively: Minneapolis and Philadelphia, 1958 and Minneapolis and Philadelphia, 1978.

15. "Constitution, 1918," *Documents,* pp. 272-276.

16. Article 7, *Augsburg Confession* in *The Book of Concord: Confessions of the Evangelical Lutheran Church,* ed. and tr. Theodore

G. Tappert et al. (Philadelphia: Muhlenberg Press, 1959), p. 32.

17. "Chicago Theses, 1919," *Documents,* pp. 298-301.

18. "Knubel-Jacobs Statement, 'The Essentials of the Catholic Spirit in the Church,' 1919," *Documents,* p. 301-312. This statement became the basis of the important "Washington Declaration" adopted by the ULCA in 1920. See *Documents,* pp. 346-355.

19. "Minneapolis Theses, 1925," *Documents,* pp. 340-342.

20. *Minutes of the First Biennial Convention of the American Lutheran Conference . . . 1932,* p. 46. These *Minutes* are printed in the *Journal of The American Lutheran Conference* 2 (March, 1937), pp. 19-47.

21. "Constitution, 1962," *Documents,* pp. 565-573.

22. Johannes Knudsen, *The Formation of the Lutheran Church in America* (Philadelphia: Fortress Press, 1978), pp. 119-120.

23. See *LCA Yearbook 1985,* ed. Reuben T. Swanson (Philadelphia: The Board of Publication of the Lutheran Church in America, 1985), p. 388.

The American Lutheran Church

1. *Luther at the Diet of Worms,* vol. 32, *Luther's Works,* American Edition, ed. Helmut T. Lehmann (Philadelphia: Fortress Press, 1958), p. 112.

2. Quoted in Theodore G. Tappert, ed., *Lutheran Confessional Theology in America, 1840–1880,* A Library of Protestant Thought (New York: Oxford University Press, 1972), p. 7.

3. Quoted in Ibid., p. 6.

4. Stauch's diary is printed in Theodore G. Tappert, "The Diaries of John Stough, 1806–1807," *The Lutheran Quarterly* 12 (February, 1960), pp. 45-50.

5. From Stauch's autobiography, quoted in Fred W. Meuser and Charles P. Lutz, "Trailblazing in the Ohio Wilderness: How Shall Frontier Ministry Be Conducted?" in *Church Roots: Stories of Nine Immigrant Groups That Became The American Lu-*

theran Church, ed. Charles P. Lutz (Minneapolis: Augsburg Publishing House, 1985), p. 30.

6. J. A. Bergh, *Den norsk lutherske Kirkes Historie i Amerika* (Minneapolis: published by author, 1914), p. 80.

7. H. G. Stub, *To Taler ved Lutherfesten den 11te November 1883, holdt i Vor Frelsers Menigheds Kirke i Minneapolis,* p. 13.

8. "Justification for Synodical Conference, 1871," *Documents,* p. 188.

9. C. F. W. Walther, "Our Common Task: The Saving of Souls— 1 Tim. 4, 16," in *The Word of His Grace; Occasional and Festival Sermons,* ed. and tr. by Evangelical Lutheran Synod Translation Committee (Lake Mills, Iowa: Graphic Publishing Company, 1978), p. 91.

10. Quoted in E. Clifford Nelson, *The Lutheran Church Among Norwegian-Americans: A History of the Evangelical Lutheran Church,* vol. 2 (Minneapolis: Augsburg Publishing House, 1960), p. 177.

11. "Doctrinal Agreements, 1906–1915," *Documents,* pp. 232-235. The *Opgjør* is sometimes referred to as the "Madison Agreement."

12. "Constitution, 1930," *Documents,* pp. 335-338.

13. See P. S. Vig, "Rapport fra to Møder," *Danskeren* 28 (5 February 1919).

14. "Minneapolis Theses, 1925," *Documents,* pp. 340-342.

15. T. F. Gullixson in his presidential report to the Conference in *Minutes of the Third Biennial Convention of the American Lutheran Conference . . . 1936,* p. 83. These *Minutes* are printed in the *Journal of The American Lutheran Conference* 2 (March, 1937), pp. 77-98.

16. "United Testimony on Faith and Life, 1952," *Documents,* pp. 498-511.

17. Ibid., p. 501.

18. "Constitution, 1958," *Documents,* p. 533.

19. Ibid., pp. 531-538.

20. See *1985 Yearbook of the American Lutheran Church,* ed. Kathryn W. Baerwald and Shirley A. Medin (Minneapolis: Augsburg Publishing House, 1985), p. 391.

The Association of Evangelical Lutheran Churches

1. Article 2 of the constitution of the Lutheran Church—Missouri Synod in *Doctrinal Declarations: A Collection of Official Statements on the Doctrinal Positions of Various Lutheran Bodies in America* (Saint Louis: Concordia Publishing House, 1957), p. 3.
2. W. J. Mann, *Lutheranism in America: An Essay on the Present Condition of the Lutheran Church in the United States* (Philadelphia: Lindsay & Blakiston, 1857), p. 85.
3. Originally published in German, it appeared in English as *Christian Dogmatics*, 4 vols., tr. Theodore Engelder et al. (Saint Louis: Concordia Publishing House, 1950-1957).
4. *Doctrinal Declarations*, pp. 43-57. See also "Brief Statement, 1932," *Documents*, pp. 381-392.
5. *Doctrinal Declarations*, p. 43.
6. The complete text of "A Statement," is reprinted in *Concordia Historical Institute Quarterly* 43 (November, 1970), pp. 150-152.
7. Roland Wiederaenders, quoted in James E. Adams, *Preus of Missouri and the Great Lutheran Civil War* (New York: Harper & Row, Publishers, Inc., 1977), p. 124.
8. *Report of the Synodical President to the Lutheran Church–Missouri Synod. . .Upon Receipt of Progress Report of the Board of Control of Concordia Seminary, St. Louis, Missouri, Relative to Its Action Taken on the Basis of the Report of the Fact Finding Committee appointed by the Synodical President, September 1, 1972.*
9. *Fact Finding or Fault Finding? An Analysis of President J. A. O. Preus' Investigation of Concordia Seminary, September 8, 1972.*
10. See *1977 Statistical Yearbook* (Saint Louis: The Lutheran Church–Missouri Synod, Department of Personnel and Statistics, 1978), p. 224.
11. See "Statistics for 1984: Lutheran Church Bodies in the United States and Canada," compiled by Alice M. Kendrick, director, and Miriam L. Wolbert, staff assistant, Records and Information Center, Lutheran Council in the U. S. A.

12. Quoted in Arthur Carl Piepkorn, *Profiles in Belief: The Religious Bodies of the United States and Canada*, vol. 2, *Protestant Denominations* (San Francisco: Harper & Row, Publishers, 1978), p. 120.

13. Ibid., p. 119.

FOR FURTHER READING

Encyclopedia of the Lutheran Church. 3 vols. Minneapolis: Augsburg, 1965. (A treasury of information about European and American Lutheranism.)*

European background

Bergendoff, Conrad. *The Church of the Lutheran Reformation: A Historical Survey of Lutheranism.* St. Louis: Concordia, 1967. (Readable and informative.)*

American religion

Hudson, Winthrop. *Religion in America: An Historical Account of the Development of American Religious Life.* 3rd ed. New York: Scribner's, 1981. (An easy introduction.)

Mead, Sidney E. *The Lively Experiment: The Shaping of Christianity in America.* New York: Harper & Row, 1963. (A book of insightful essays.)

American Lutheranism

Flesner, Dorris A. *American Lutherans Help Shape World Council: The Role of the Lutheran Churches of America in the Formation of the World Council of Churches.* Lutheran Historical Conference Publication no. 2. Dubuque, Iowa: Brown, 1981.

---

*An asterisk indicates a title that is out of print. These volumes are almost always available in large Lutheran libraries.

Nelson, E. Clifford. *Lutheranism in North America, 1914–1970.*
Minneapolis: Augsburg, 1972. (Focuses on Lutheran unity.)*

Nelson, E. Clifford. *The Rise of World Lutheranism: An American Perspective.* Philadelphia: Fortress, 1982. (About the emergence of the Lutheran World Federation and American contributions to that story.)

Nelson, E. Clifford. *The Lutherans in North America.* rev. ed. Philadelphia: Fortress, 1980. (*The* book. It belongs in every congregation's library.)*

Thorkelson, Willmar. *Lutherans in the U.S.A.* Rev. ed. Minneapolis: Augsburg, 1978. (A booklet emphasizing events of recent years.)*

Tiejten, John H. *Which Way to Lutheran Unity?* St. Louis: Clayton, 1975. (A scholarly study of approaches to Lutheran unity.)

Wiederaenders, Robert C. and Tillmanns, Walter G. *The Synods of American Lutheranism.* Lutheran Historical Conference, Publication no. 1. St. Louis: Concordia Seminary, 1968. (Includes official names, brief data, and bibliography on American Lutheran bodies.)

Wentz, Abdel Ross. *A Basic History of Lutheranism in America.* Rev. ed. Philadelphia: Fortress, 1964. (A look at the whole story.)*

Wentz, Frederick K. *Lutherans in Concert: The Story of the National Lutheran Council, 1918–1966.* Minneapolis: Augsburg, 1968.*

Wolf, Richard C. *Documents of Lutheran Unity in America.* Philadelphia: Fortress, 1966.*

Wolf, Richard C. *Lutherans in North America.* Philadelphia: Lutheran Church Press, 1965. (Popular and easy to read.)*

The Lutheran Church in America

(The general histories mentioned above concentrate heavily on the story of eastern Lutheranism.)

Arden, G. Everett. *Augustana Heritage: A History of the Augustana Evangelical Lutheran Church.* Rock Island, Ill.: Augustana Press, 1963.*

Jacobs, Henry E. *A History of the Evangelical Lutheran Church in the United States.* New York: Scribner's, 1902. (An older book containing a wealth of information about the traditions contributing to the ULCA. Although currently out of print, in 1986 AMS Pr., Inc., of New York announced plans to reprint the 1893 edition.)*

Jalkanen, Ralph J. *The Faith of the Finns: Historical Perspectives on the Finnish Lutheran Church in America.* East Lansing, Mich.: Michigan State University, 1972.

Knudsen, Johannes. *The Formation of the Lutheran Church in America.* Philadelphia: Fortress, 1978. (About the merger creating the LCA.)*

Mortensen, Enok. *The Danish Lutheran Church in America: The History and Heritage of the American Evangelical Lutheran Church.* Philadelphia: Board of Publication, LCA, 1967.*

The American Lutheran Church

Buehring, P. H. *The Spirit of the American Lutheran Church.* Columbus: Lutheran Book Concern, 1940. (A book about the "old" ALC, including sketches of the antecedent bodies.)*

Fevold, Eugene L. *The Lutheran Free Church: A Fellowship of American Lutheran Congregations, 1897–1963.* Minneapolis: Augsburg, 1969.

Jensen, John M. *The United Evangelical Lutheran Church: An Interpretation.* Minneapolis: Augsburg, 1964.*

Lutz, Charles P., ed. *Church Roots: Stories of Nine Immigrant Groups That Became The American Lutheran Church.* Minneapolis: Augsburg, 1985.

Meuser, Fred W. *The Formation of the American Lutheran Church: A Case Study in Lutheran Unity.* Columbus: Wartburg Press, 1958. (A scholarly study of the merger creating the "Old" ALC.)*

Nelson, E. Clifford and Fevold, Eugene L. *The Lutheran Church among Norwegian-Americans.* 2 vols. Minneapolis: Augsburg, 1960.*

The Association of Evangelical Lutheran Churches

Adams, James E. *Preus of Missouri and the Great Lutheran Civil War*. New York: Harper & Row, 1977. (Written by a St. Louis journalist.)*

Baepler, Walter A. *A Century of Grace: A History of the Missouri Synod, 1847–1947*. St. Louis: Concordia, 1947. (Centennial history of Missouri.)*

Danker, Frederick W. *No Room in the Brotherhood: The Preus-Otten Purge of Missouri*. St. Louis: Clayton, 1977. (Written by a member of the AELC.)

Marquart, Kurt E. *Anatomy of an Explosion: A Theological Analysis of the Missouri Synod Conflict*. Grand Rapids: Baker, 1978. (Written by a member of Missouri.)

Weisheit, Eldon. *The Zeal of His House: Five Generations of Lutheran Church–Missouri Synod History (1847–1972)*. St. Louis. Concordia, 1973. (Popular and entertaining.)